the BOOKS of MAGIC
Transformations

John Ney Rieber
Writer

Peter Gross
Artist

rilyn van Valkenburgh   **Nathan Eyring**
Colorists

Richard Starkings and Comicraft
Letterer

rilyn van Valkenburgh   **Michael Kaluta**

August Hall   **Chris Bachalo**
Original Covers

Neil Gaiman
Consultant

Timothy Hunter & The Books of Magic
created by
Neil Gaiman & John Bolton

Table of Contents

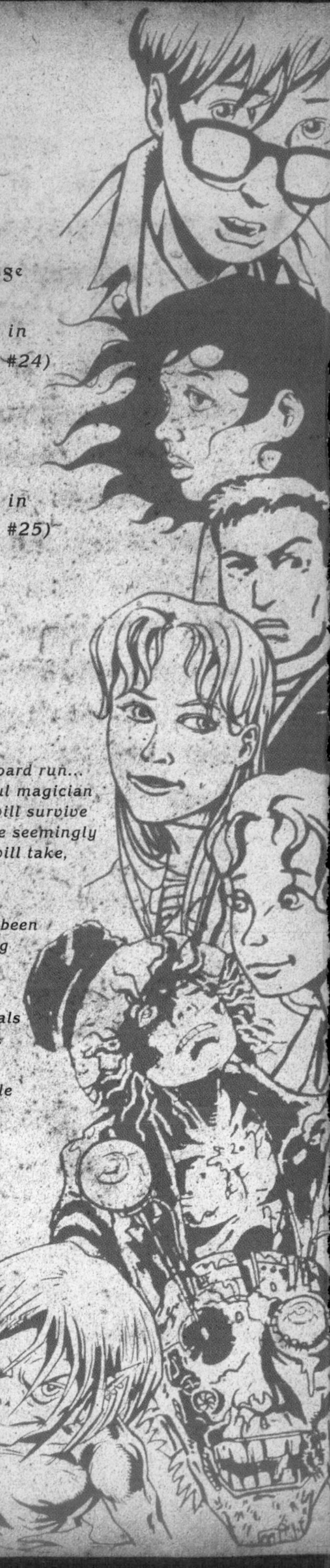

Dramatis Personae

Timothy Hunter

An average teenager whose greatest aspiration was a perfect skateboard run... until he learned that he had the potential to become the most powerful magician in history. Tim has yet to accept his destiny, and it's uncertain he will survive to claim it. But all around him, powerful forces have emerged — some seemingly content to watch and wait to see what form his magical heritage will take, others seeking a more direct role in Tim's ultimate fate.

Molly

Tim's classmate and girlfriend. Her relationship with Tim has been tested by a recent trip to Hell, where she learned disquieting things about him.

William Hunter

Tim's father — or is he? — who must endure not only the trials of raising a teenager alone, but the perils of magic as well.

Gwendolyn

A young lady from Victorian times, whose skill with a needle and thread is but one of her gifts.

Marya

A girl from the mystical realm called Free Country, haven for abused and unwanted children.

Daniel

A child banished from Free Country, tortured by his unrequited love for Marya and transformed by Reverend Slaggingham into the Climbing Boy.

Reverend Slaggingham

Originally from Victorian England, the Reverend's head is all that remains of this scheming cyborg.

The Amadan

Fool, jester, and string-puller par excellence of the Faerie realm.

Death

One of the Endless. Sister to Dream.

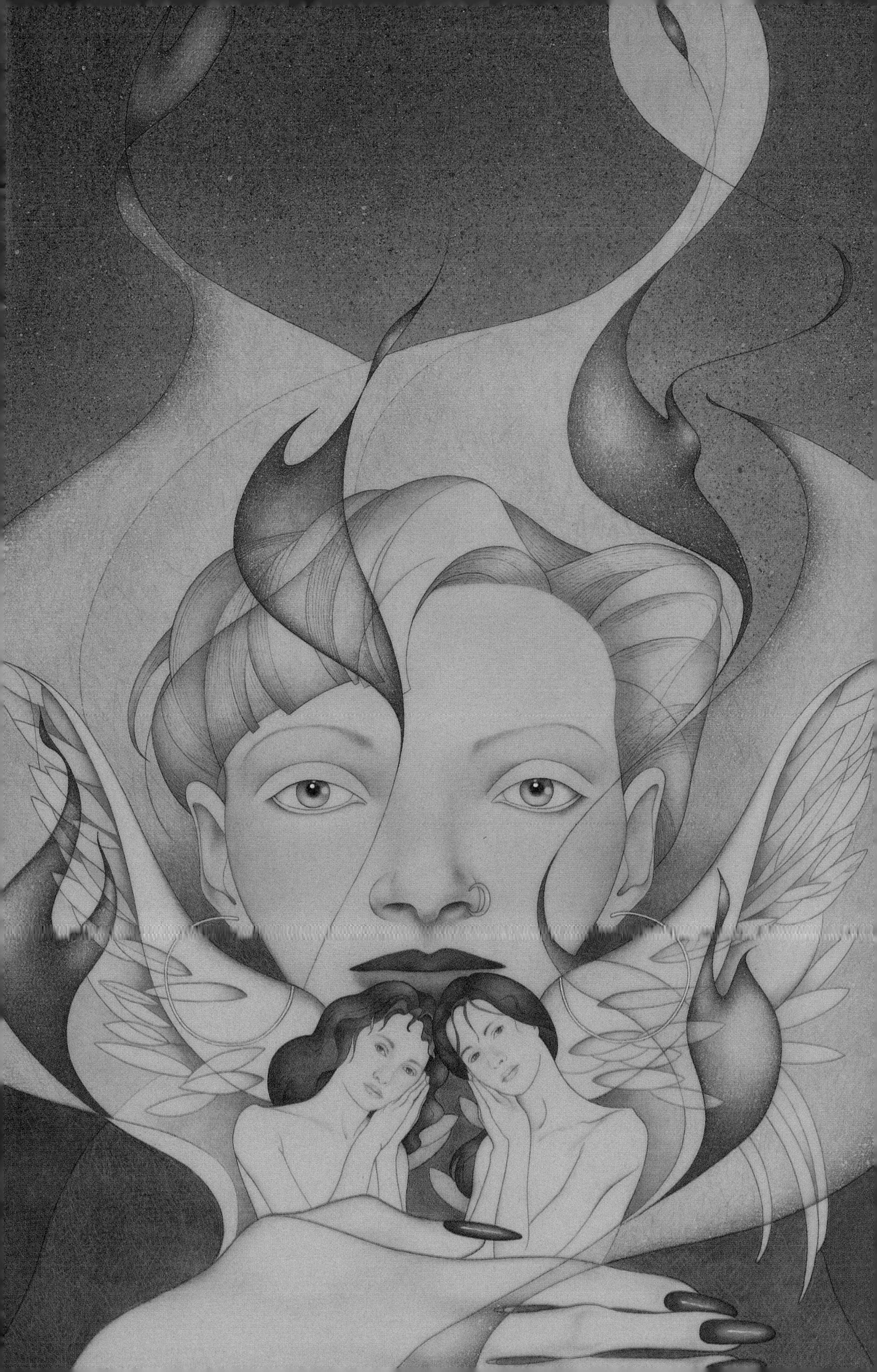

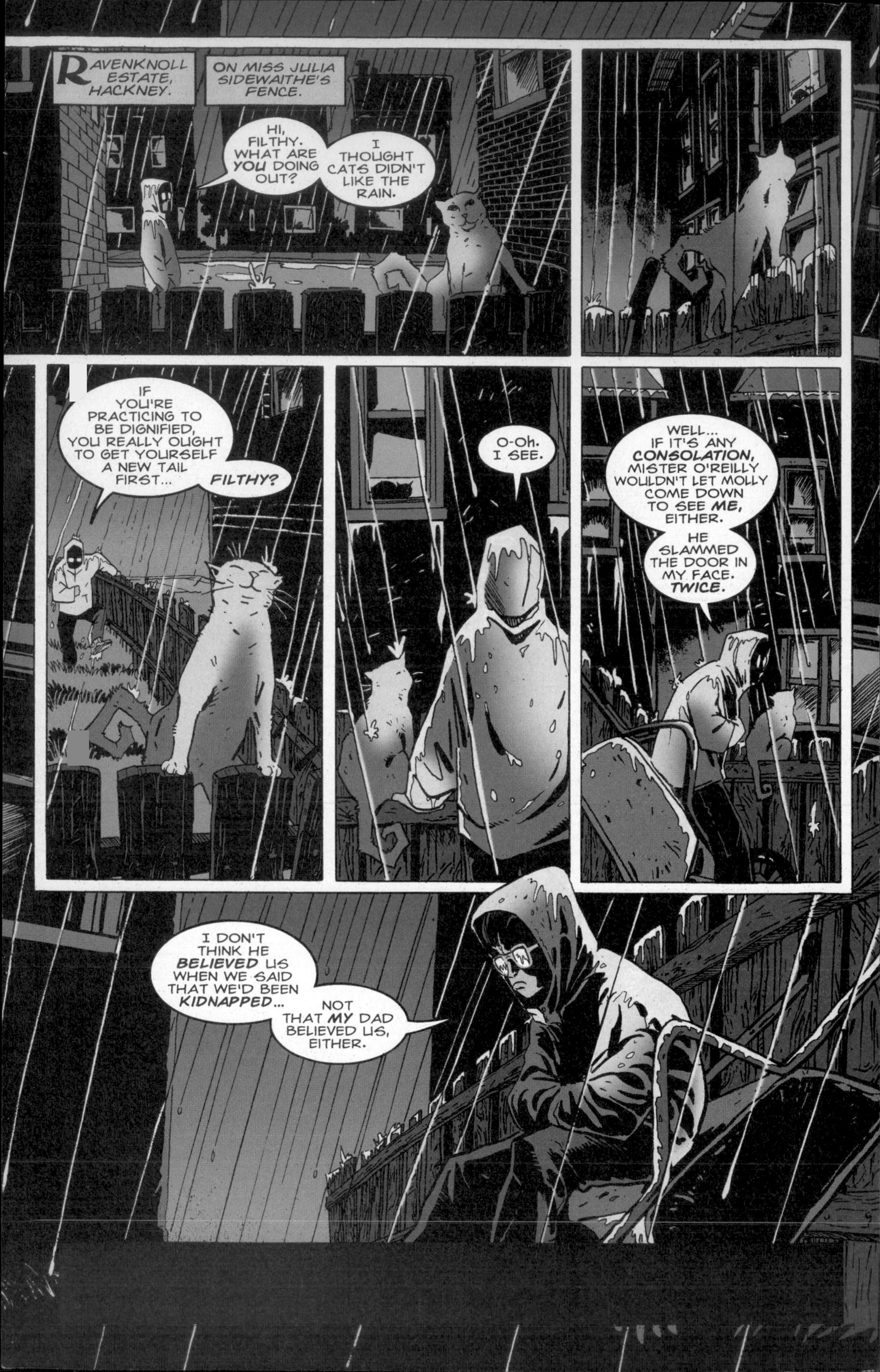
RAVENKNOLL ESTATE, HACKNEY.
ON MISS JULIA SIDEWAITHE'S FENCE.
HI, FILTHY. WHAT ARE YOU DOING OUT?
I THOUGHT CATS DIDN'T LIKE THE RAIN.
IF YOU'RE PRACTICING TO BE DIGNIFIED, YOU REALLY OUGHT TO GET YOURSELF A NEW TAIL FIRST... FILTHY?
O-OH. I SEE.
WELL... IF IT'S ANY CONSOLATION, MISTER O'REILLY WOULDN'T LET MOLLY COME DOWN TO SEE ME, EITHER.
HE SLAMMED THE DOOR IN MY FACE. TWICE.
I DON'T THINK HE BELIEVED US WHEN WE SAID THAT WE'D BEEN KIDNAPPED...
NOT THAT MY DAD BELIEVED US, EITHER.

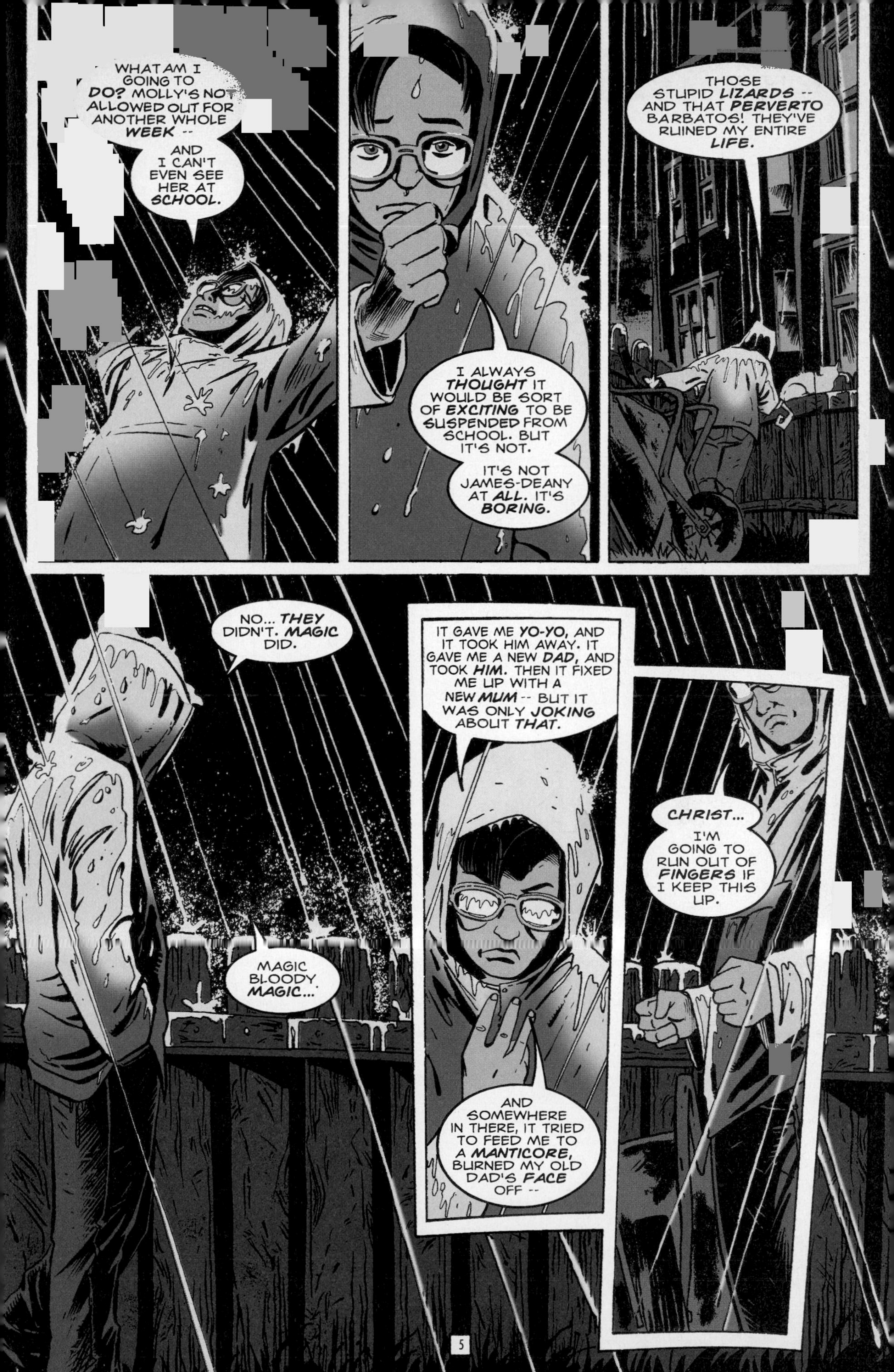
WHAT AM I GOING TO DO? MOLLY'S NOT ALLOWED OUT FOR ANOTHER WHOLE WEEK --
AND I CAN'T EVEN SEE HER AT SCHOOL.
I ALWAYS THOUGHT IT WOULD BE SORT OF EXCITING TO BE SUSPENDED FROM SCHOOL. BUT IT'S NOT.
IT'S NOT JAMES-DEANY AT ALL. IT'S BORING.
THOSE STUPID LIZARDS -- AND THAT PERVERTO BARBATOS! THEY'VE RUINED MY ENTIRE LIFE.
NO... THEY DIDN'T. MAGIC DID.
MAGIC BLOODY MAGIC...
IT GAVE ME YO-YO, AND IT TOOK HIM AWAY. IT GAVE ME A NEW DAD, AND TOOK HIM. THEN IT FIXED ME UP WITH A NEW MUM -- BUT IT WAS ONLY JOKING ABOUT THAT.
AND SOMEWHERE IN THERE, IT TRIED TO FEED ME TO A MANTICORE, BURNED MY OLD DAD'S FACE OFF --
CHRIST...
I'M GOING TO RUN OUT OF FINGERS IF I KEEP THIS UP.

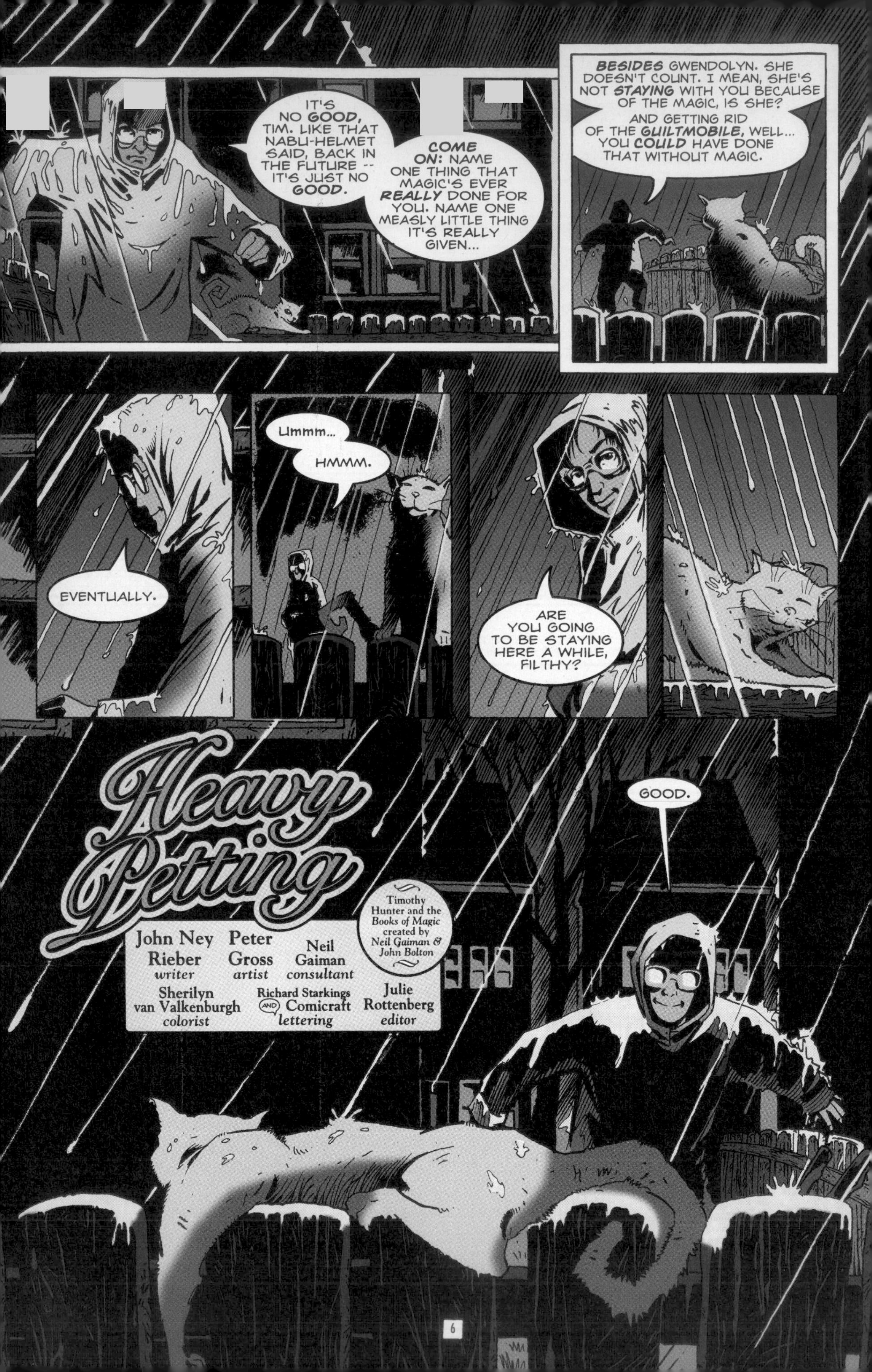
IT'S NO GOOD, TIM. LIKE THAT NABU-HELMET SAID, BACK IN THE FUTURE -- IT'S JUST NO GOOD.
COME ON: NAME ONE THING THAT MAGIC'S EVER REALLY DONE FOR YOU. NAME ONE MEASLY LITTLE THING IT'S REALLY GIVEN...
BESIDES GWENDOLYN. SHE DOESN'T COUNT. I MEAN, SHE'S NOT STAYING WITH YOU BECAUSE OF THE MAGIC, IS SHE?
AND GETTING RID OF THE GUILTMOBILE, WELL... YOU COULD HAVE DONE THAT WITHOUT MAGIC.
EVENTUALLY.
Ummm...
HMMM.
ARE YOU GOING TO BE STAYING HERE A WHILE, FILTHY?
GOOD.
Heavy Petting
John Ney Rieber writer
Peter Gross artist
Neil Gaiman consultant
Timothy Hunter and the Books of Magic created by Neil Gaiman & John Bolton
Sherilyn van Valkenburgh colorist
Richard Starkings AND Comicraft lettering
Julie Rottenberg editor

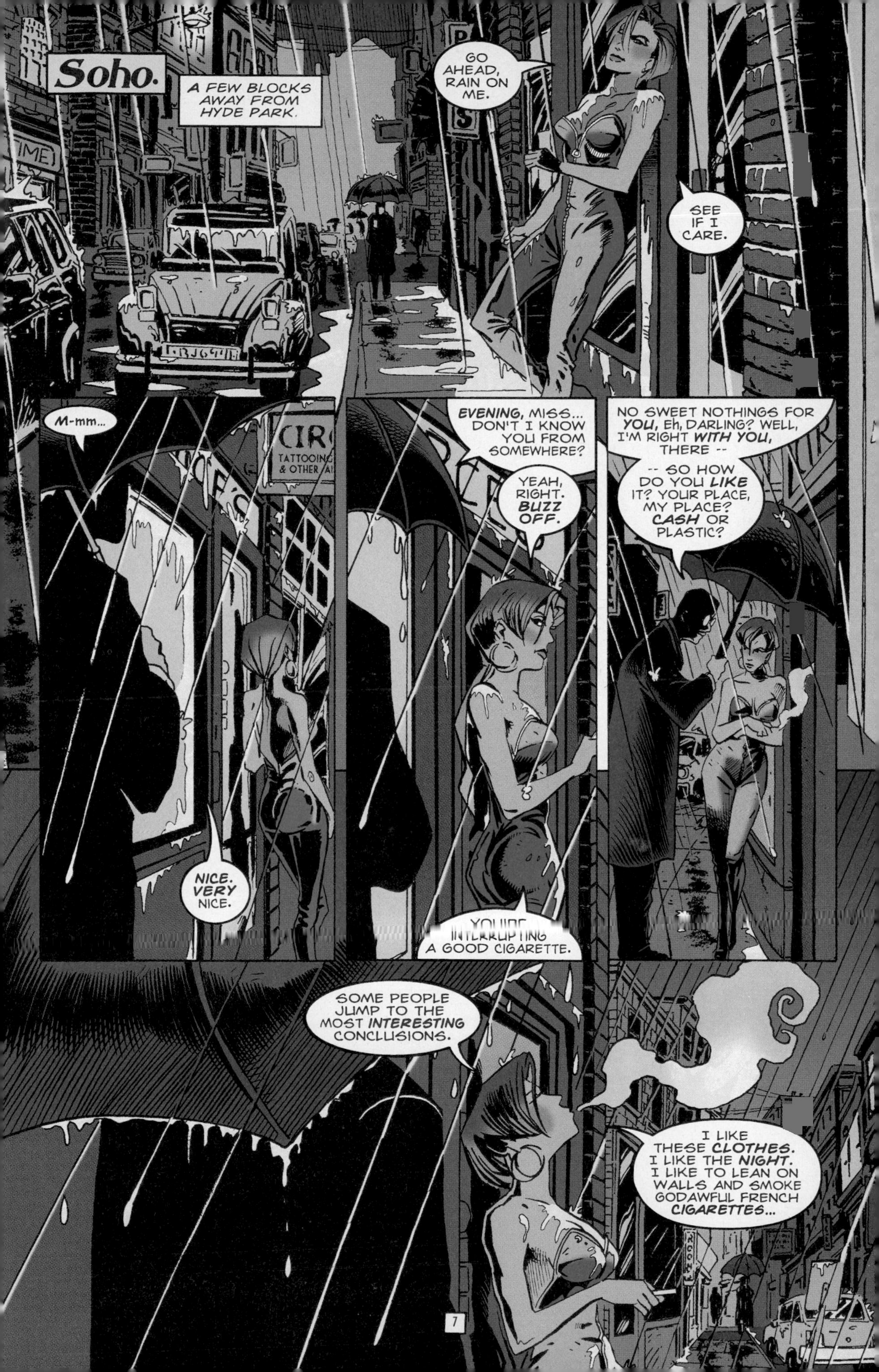
Soho.
A FEW BLOCKS AWAY FROM HYDE PARK.
GO AHEAD, RAIN ON ME.
SEE IF I CARE.
M-mm...
NICE. VERY NICE.
EVENING, MISS... DON'T I KNOW YOU FROM SOMEWHERE?
YEAH, RIGHT. BUZZ OFF.
YOU'RE INTERRUPTING A GOOD CIGARETTE.
NO SWEET NOTHINGS FOR YOU, Eh, DARLING? WELL, I'M RIGHT WITH YOU, THERE --
-- SO HOW DO YOU LIKE IT? YOUR PLACE, MY PLACE? CASH OR PLASTIC?
SOME PEOPLE JUMP TO THE MOST INTERESTING CONCLUSIONS.
I LIKE THESE CLOTHES. I LIKE THE NIGHT. I LIKE TO LEAN ON WALLS AND SMOKE GODAWFUL FRENCH CIGARETTES...

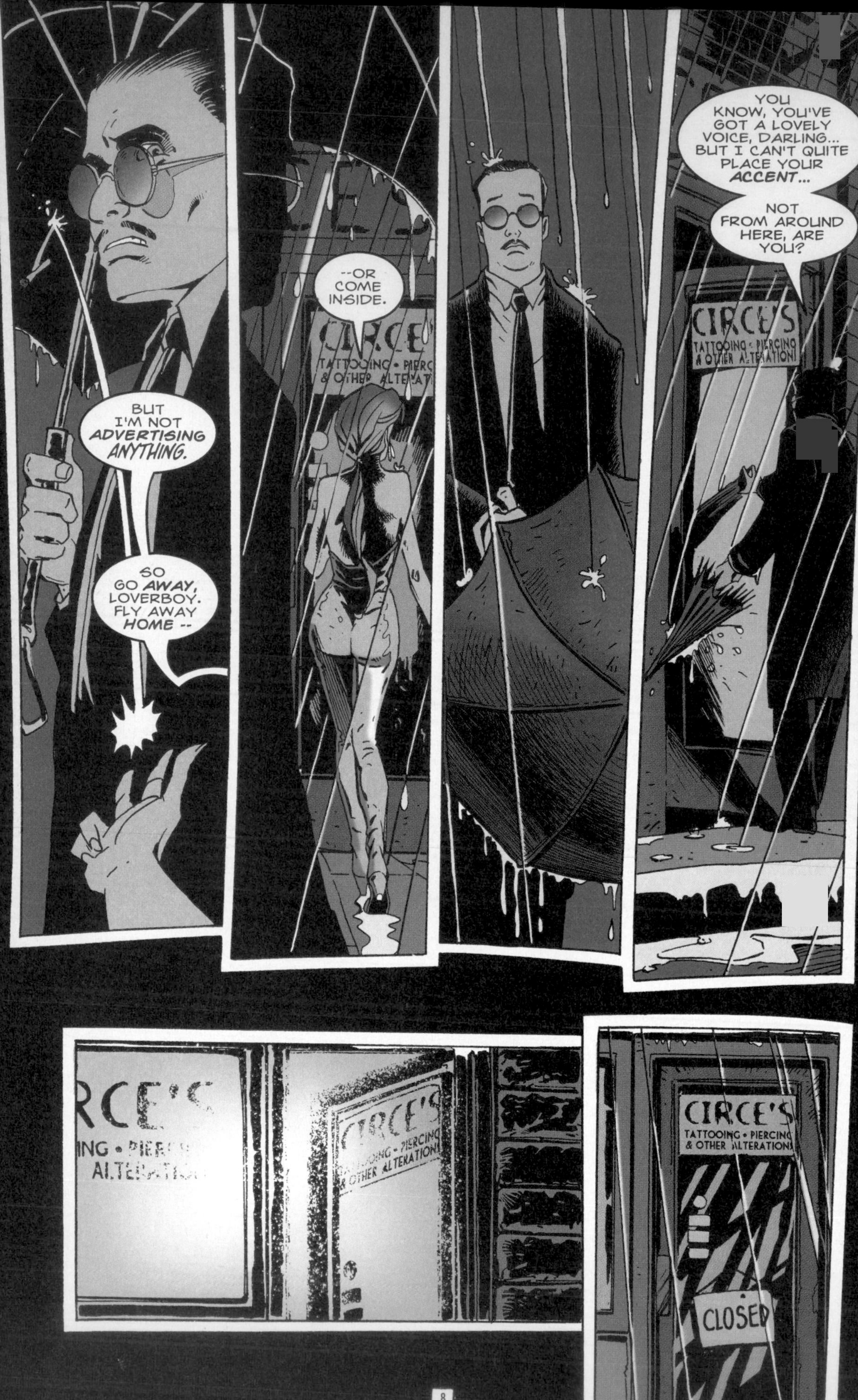
BUT I'M NOT ADVERTISING ANYTHING.
SO GO AWAY, LOVERBOY. FLY AWAY HOME --
--OR COME INSIDE.
CIRCE'S
YOU KNOW, YOU'VE GOT A LOVELY VOICE, DARLING... BUT I CAN'T QUITE PLACE YOUR ACCENT...
NOT FROM AROUND HERE, ARE YOU?
CIRCE'S
TATTOOING • PIERCING & OTHER ALTERATIONS
CLOSED

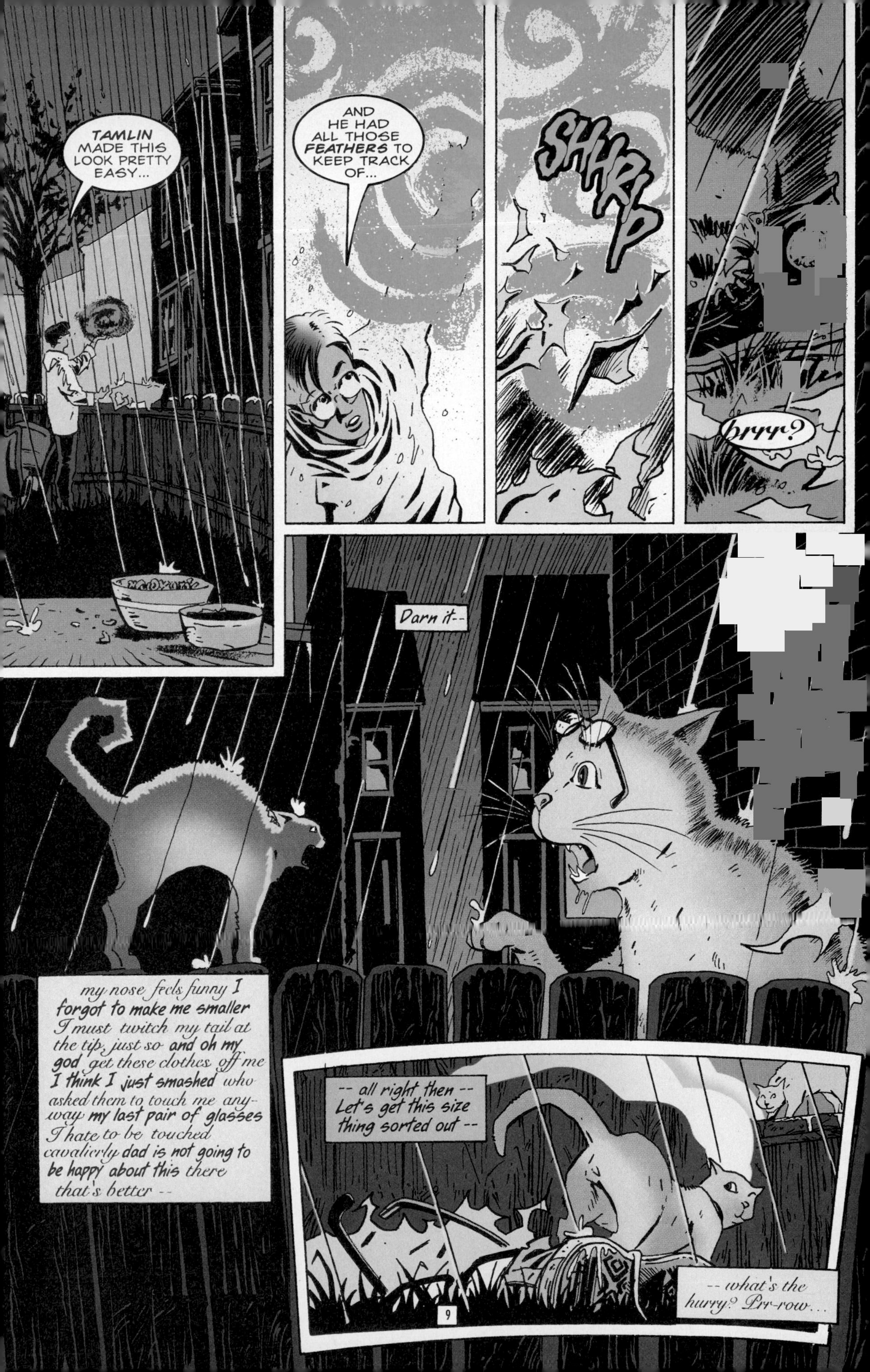
TAMLIN MADE THIS LOOK PRETTY EASY...
AND HE HAD ALL THOSE FEATHERS TO KEEP TRACK OF...
SHHRIP
brrr?
Darn it--
my nose feels funny I forgot to make me smaller I must twitch my tail at the tip, just so and oh my god get these clothes off me I think I just smashed who asked them to touch me any-way my last pair of glasses I hate to be touched cavalierly dad is not going to be happy about this there that's better --
-- all right then -- Let's get this size thing sorted out --
-- what's the hurry? Prr-row...

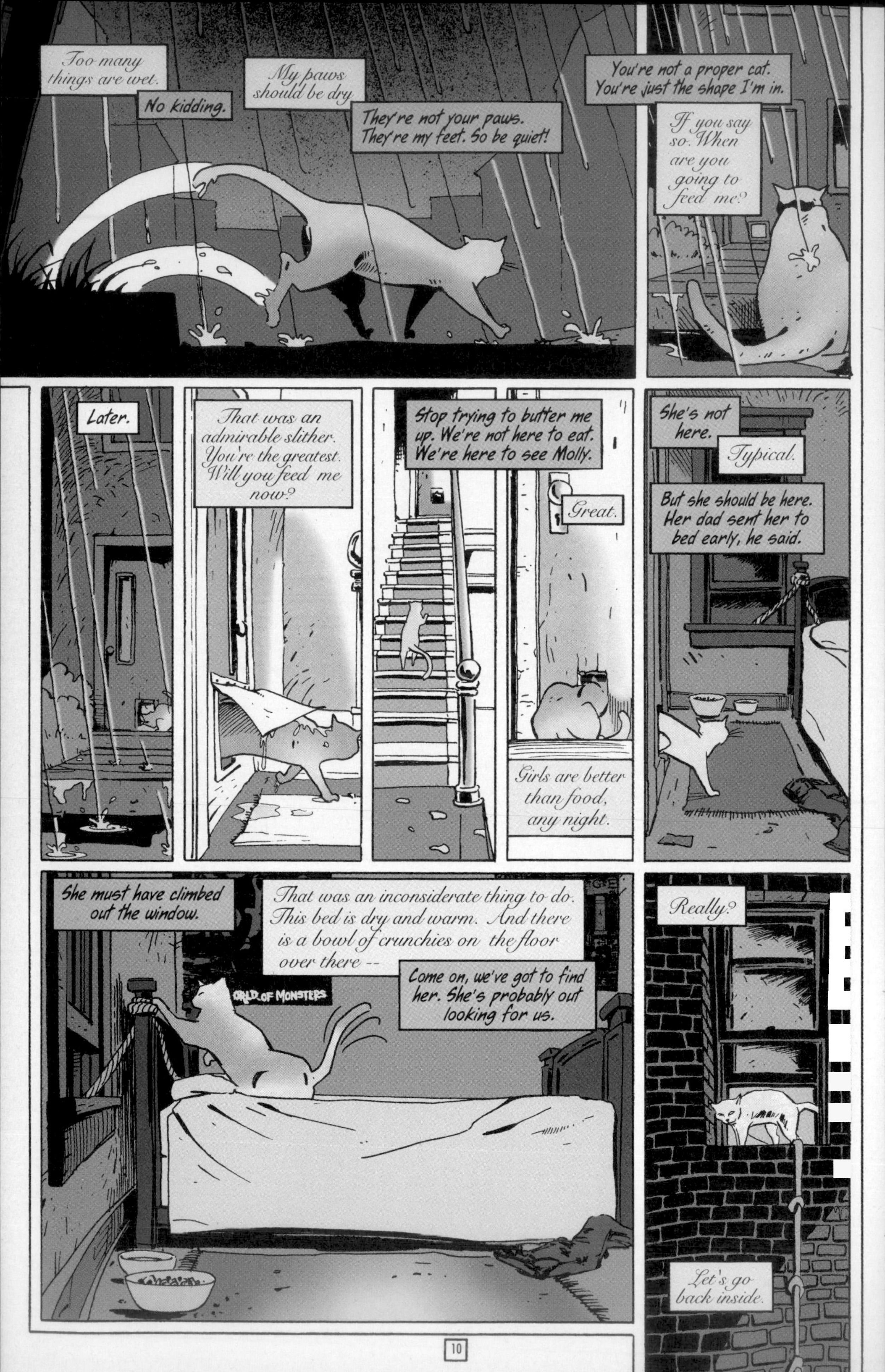
Too many things are wet.
No kidding.
My paws should be dry.
They're not your paws. They're my feet. So be quiet!
You're not a proper cat. You're just the shape I'm in.
If you say so. When are you going to feed me?
Later.
That was an admirable slither. You're the greatest. Will you feed me now?
Stop trying to butter me up. We're not here to eat. We're here to see Molly.
Great.
Girls are better than food, any night.
She's not here.
Typical.
But she should be here. Her dad sent her to bed early, he said.
She must have climbed out the window.
That was an inconsiderate thing to do. This bed is dry and warm. And there is a bowl of crunchies on the floor over there --
Come on, we've got to find her. She's probably out looking for us.
Really?
Let's go back inside.

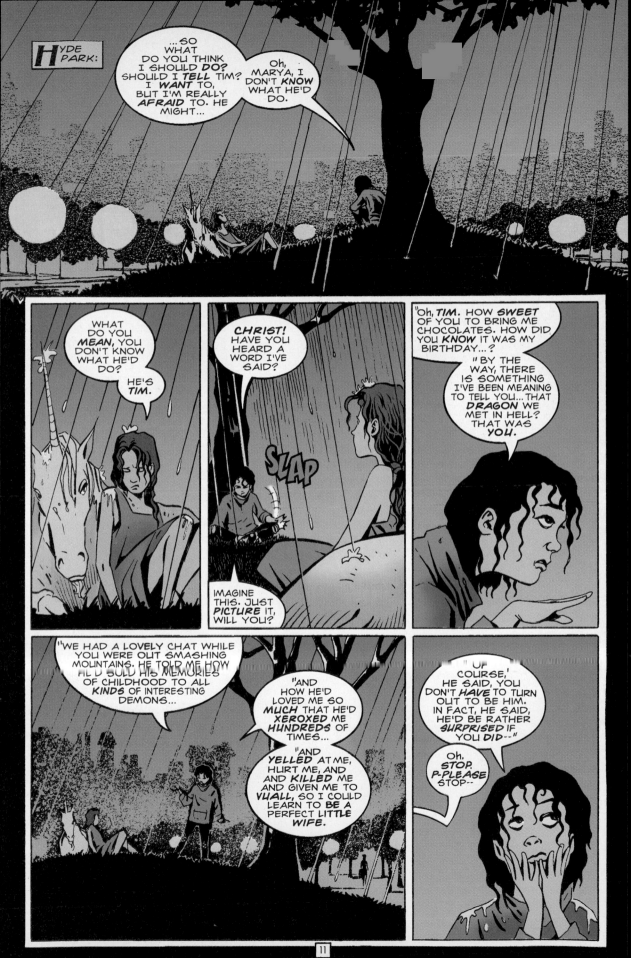

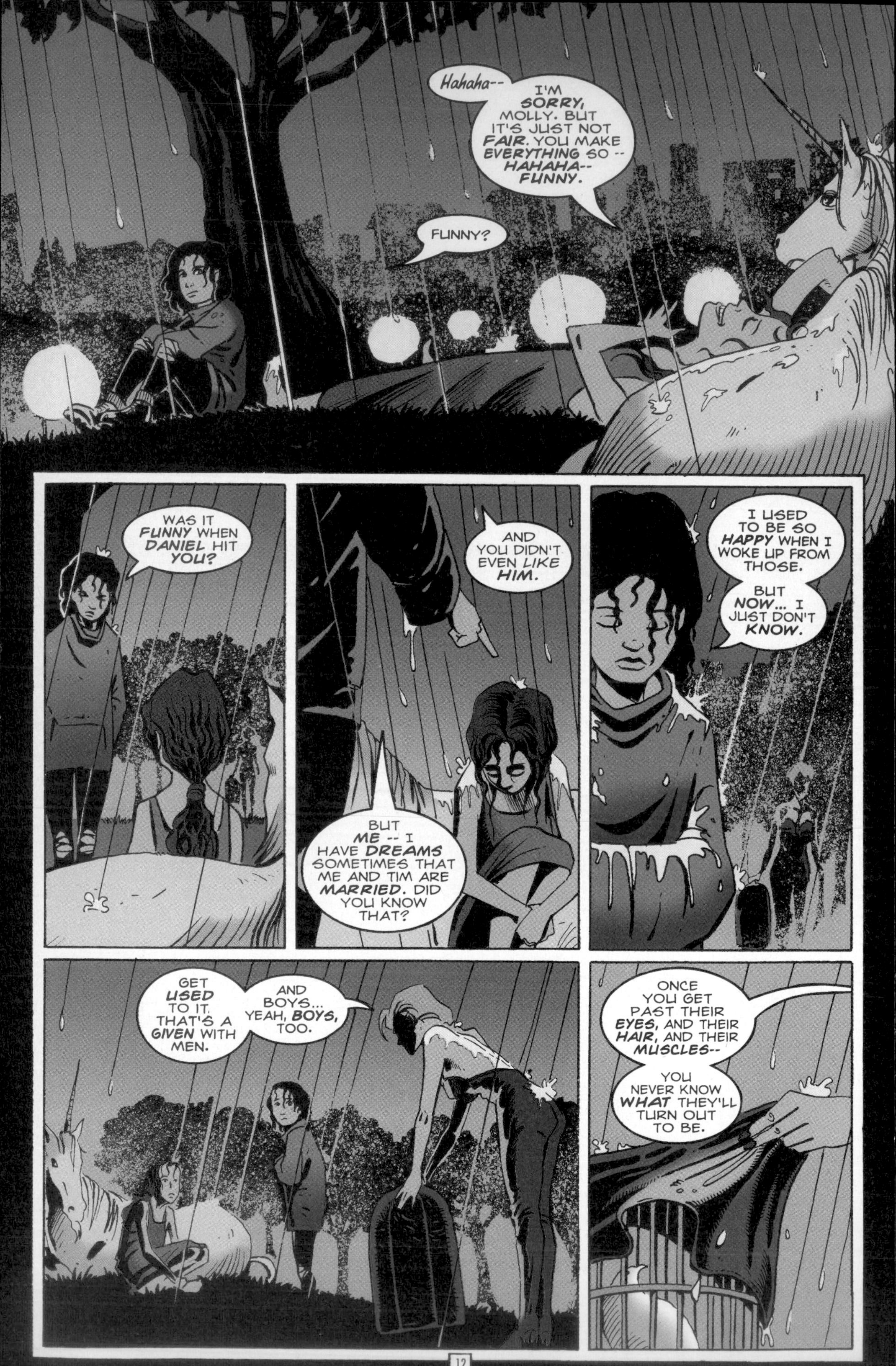
Hahaha--
I'M SORRY, MOLLY. BUT IT'S JUST NOT FAIR. YOU MAKE EVERYTHING SO -- HAHAHA-- FUNNY.
FUNNY?
WAS IT FUNNY WHEN DANIEL HIT YOU?
AND YOU DIDN'T EVEN LIKE HIM.
BUT ME -- I HAVE DREAMS SOMETIMES THAT ME AND TIM ARE MARRIED. DID YOU KNOW THAT?
I USED TO BE SO HAPPY WHEN I WOKE UP FROM THOSE.
BUT NOW... I JUST DON'T KNOW.
GET USED TO IT. THAT'S A GIVEN WITH MEN.
AND BOYS... YEAH, BOYS, TOO.
ONCE YOU GET PAST THEIR EYES, AND THEIR HAIR, AND THEIR MUSCLES--
YOU NEVER KNOW WHAT THEY'LL TURN OUT TO BE.

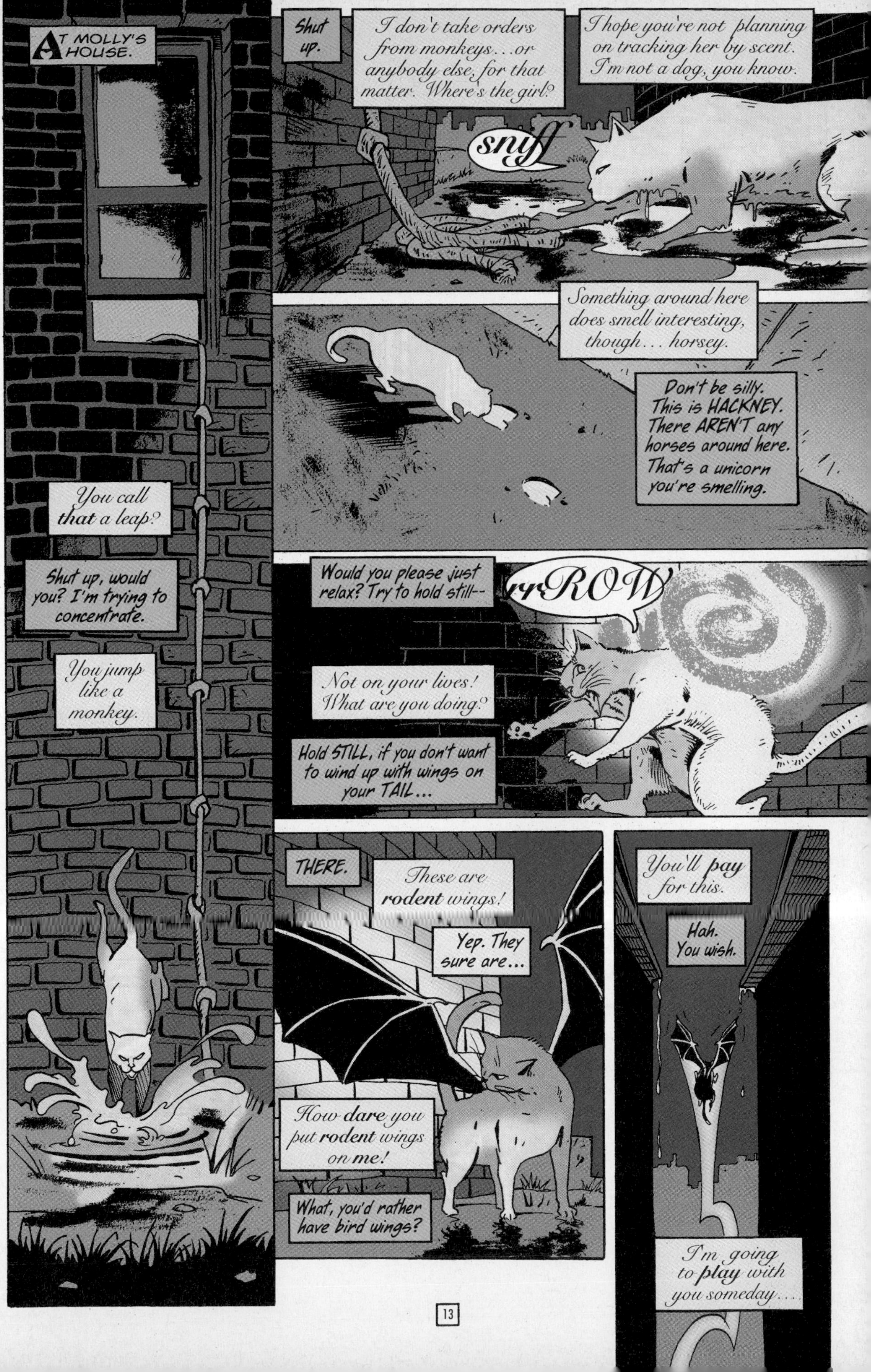

At Molly's house.
Shut up.
I don't take orders from monkeys...or anybody else, for that matter. Where's the girl?
I hope you're not planning on tracking her by scent. I'm not a dog, you know.
sniff
Something around here does smell interesting, though... horsey.
Don't be silly. This is HACKNEY. There AREN'T any horses around here. That's a unicorn you're smelling.
You call that a leap?
Shut up, would you? I'm trying to concentrate.
You jump like a monkey.
Would you please just relax? Try to hold still--
rrROW
Not on your lives! What are you doing?
Hold STILL, if you don't want to wind up with wings on your TAIL...
THERE.
These are rodent wings!
Yep. They sure are...
How dare you put rodent wings on me!
What, you'd rather have bird wings?
You'll pay for this.
Hah. You wish.
I'm going to play with you someday...

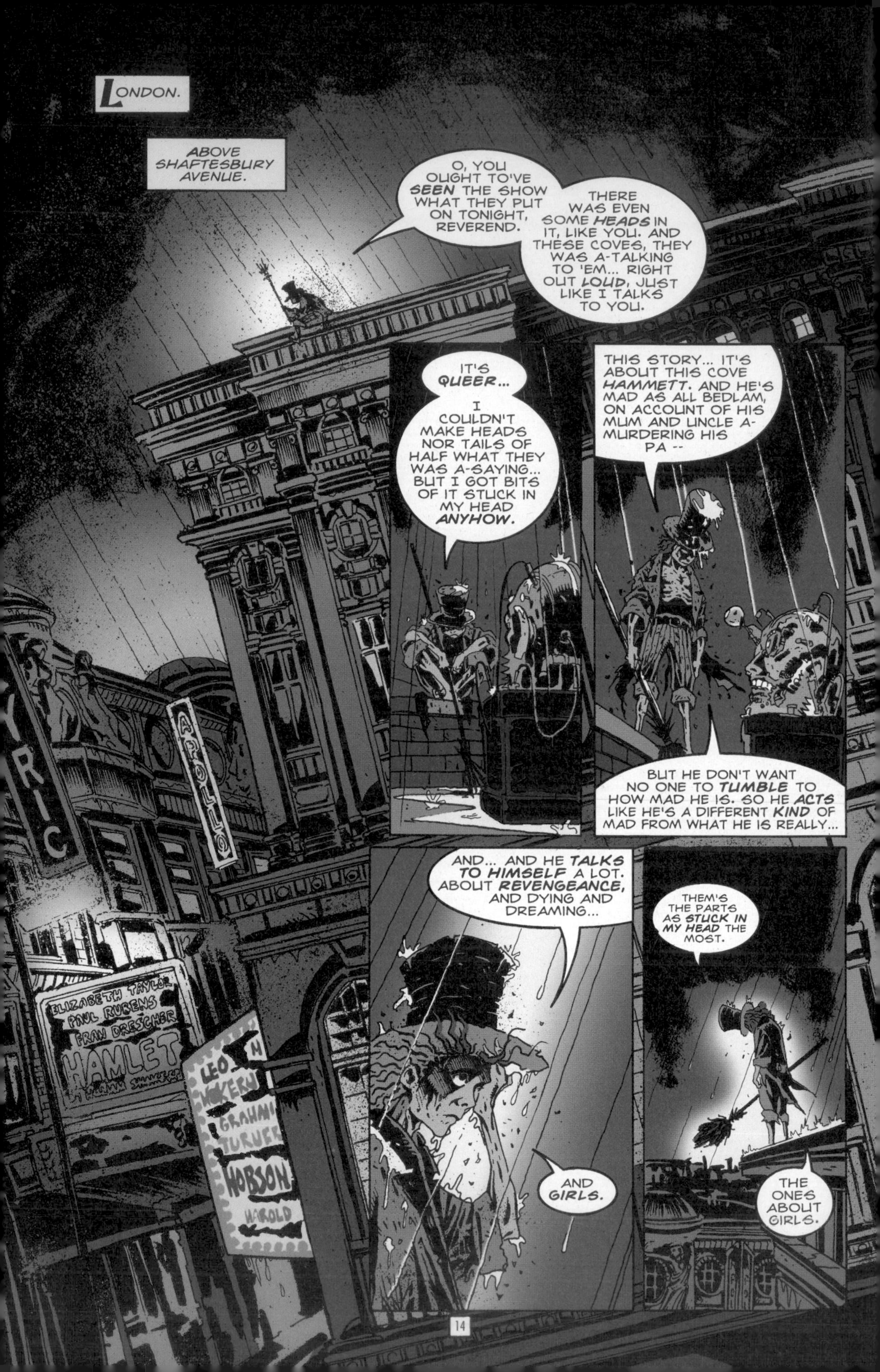
LONDON.
ABOVE SHAFTESBURY AVENUE.
O, YOU OUGHT TO'VE SEEN THE SHOW WHAT THEY PUT ON TONIGHT, REVEREND.
THERE WAS EVEN SOME HEADS IN IT, LIKE YOU. AND THESE COVES, THEY WAS A-TALKING TO 'EM... RIGHT OUT LOUD, JUST LIKE I TALKS TO YOU.
APOLLO
ELIZABETH TAYLOR
PAUL RUBENS
FRAN DRESCHER
HAMLET
IT'S QUEER...
I COULDN'T MAKE HEADS NOR TAILS OF HALF WHAT THEY WAS A-SAYING... BUT I GOT BITS OF IT STUCK IN MY HEAD ANYHOW.
THIS STORY... IT'S ABOUT THIS COVE HAMMETT. AND HE'S MAD AS ALL BEDLAM, ON ACCOUNT OF HIS MUM AND UNCLE A-MURDERING HIS PA --
BUT HE DON'T WANT NO ONE TO TUMBLE TO HOW MAD HE IS. SO HE ACTS LIKE HE'S A DIFFERENT KIND OF MAD FROM WHAT HE IS REALLY...
AND... AND HE TALKS TO HIMSELF A LOT. ABOUT REVENGEANCE, AND DYING AND DREAMING...
AND GIRLS.
THEM'S THE PARTS AS STUCK IN MY HEAD THE MOST.
THE ONES ABOUT GIRLS.

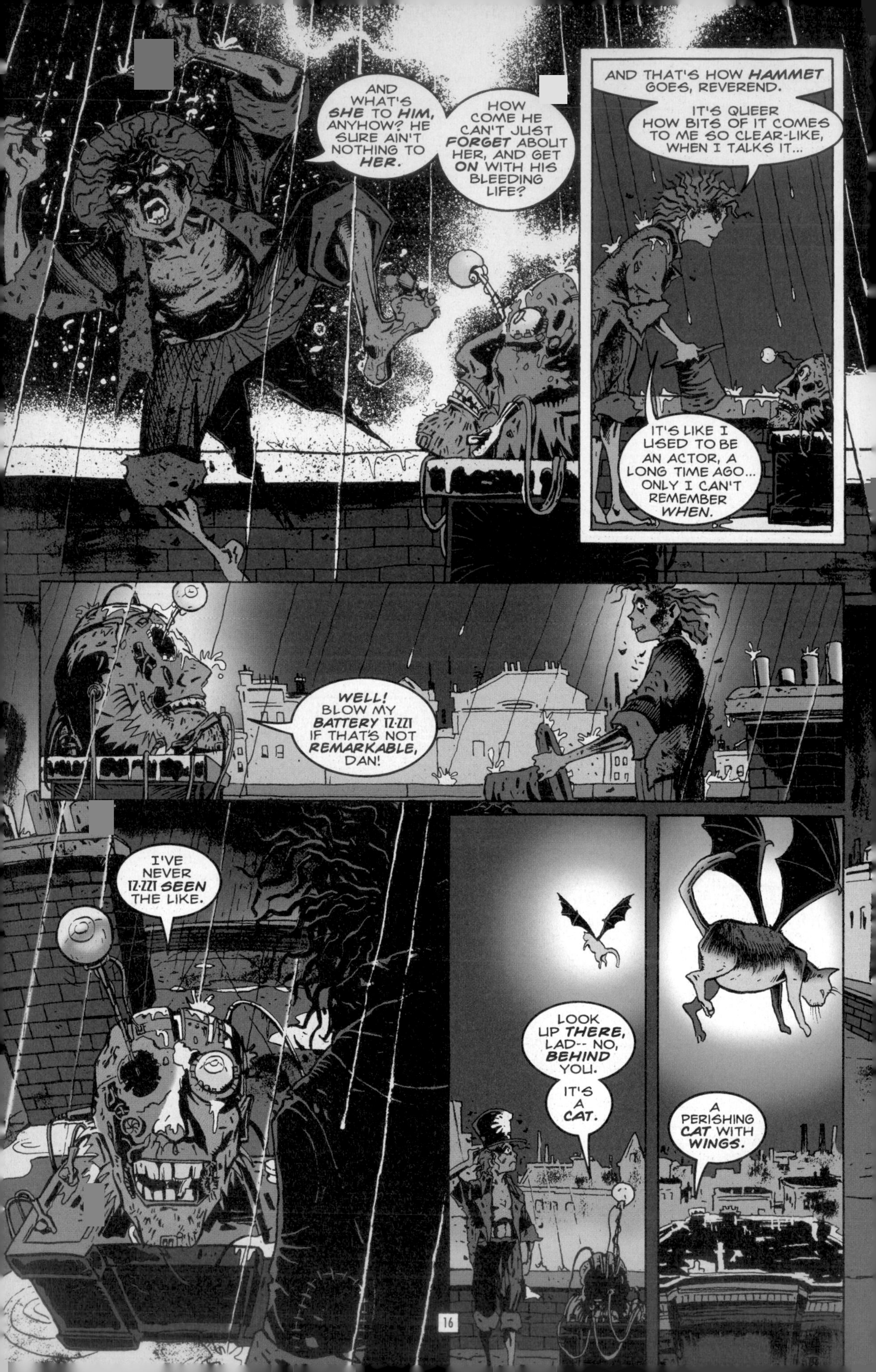
AND WHAT'S SHE TO HIM, ANYHOW? HE SURE AIN'T NOTHING TO HER.
HOW COME HE CAN'T JUST FORGET ABOUT HER, AND GET ON WITH HIS BLEEDING LIFE?
AND THAT'S HOW HAMMET GOES, REVEREND.
IT'S QUEER HOW BITS OF IT COMES TO ME SO CLEAR-LIKE, WHEN I TALKS IT...
IT'S LIKE I USED TO BE AN ACTOR, A LONG TIME AGO... ONLY I CAN'T REMEMBER WHEN.
WELL! BLOW MY BATTERY IZ-ZZI IF THAT'S NOT REMARKABLE, DAN!
I'VE NEVER IZ-ZZI SEEN THE LIKE.
LOOK UP THERE, LAD-- NO, BEHIND YOU.
IT'S A CAT.
A PERISHING CAT WITH WINGS.

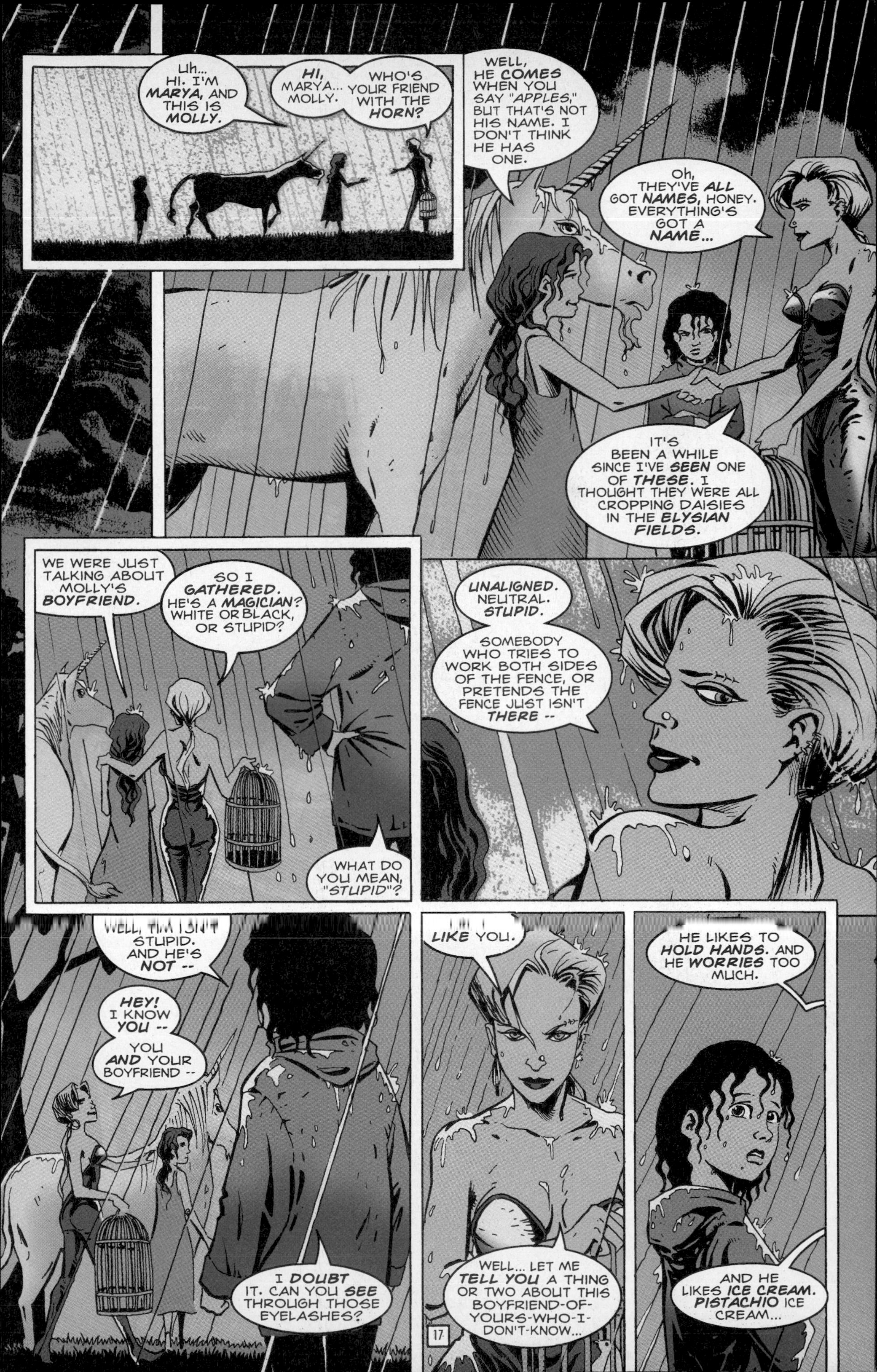
UH... HI. I'M MARYA, AND THIS IS MOLLY.
HI, MARYA... MOLLY.
WHO'S YOUR FRIEND WITH THE HORN?
WELL, HE COMES WHEN YOU SAY "APPLES," BUT THAT'S NOT HIS NAME. I DON'T THINK HE HAS ONE.
OH, THEY'VE ALL GOT NAMES, HONEY. EVERYTHING'S GOT A NAME...
IT'S BEEN A WHILE SINCE I'VE SEEN ONE OF THESE. I THOUGHT THEY WERE ALL CROPPING DAISIES IN THE ELYSIAN FIELDS.
WE WERE JUST TALKING ABOUT MOLLY'S BOYFRIEND.
SO I GATHERED. HE'S A MAGICIAN? WHITE OR BLACK, OR STUPID?
WHAT DO YOU MEAN, "STUPID"?
UNALIGNED. NEUTRAL. STUPID.
SOMEBODY WHO TRIES TO WORK BOTH SIDES OF THE FENCE, OR PRETENDS THE FENCE JUST ISN'T THERE --
WELL, TIM ISN'T STUPID. AND HE'S NOT --
HEY! I KNOW YOU --
YOU AND YOUR BOYFRIEND --
I DOUBT IT. CAN YOU SEE THROUGH THOSE EYELASHES?
LIKE YOU.
WELL... LET ME TELL YOU A THING OR TWO ABOUT THIS BOYFRIEND-OF-YOURS-WHO-I-DON'T-KNOW...
HE LIKES TO HOLD HANDS. AND HE WORRIES TOO MUCH.
AND HE LIKES ICE CREAM. PISTACHIO ICE CREAM...

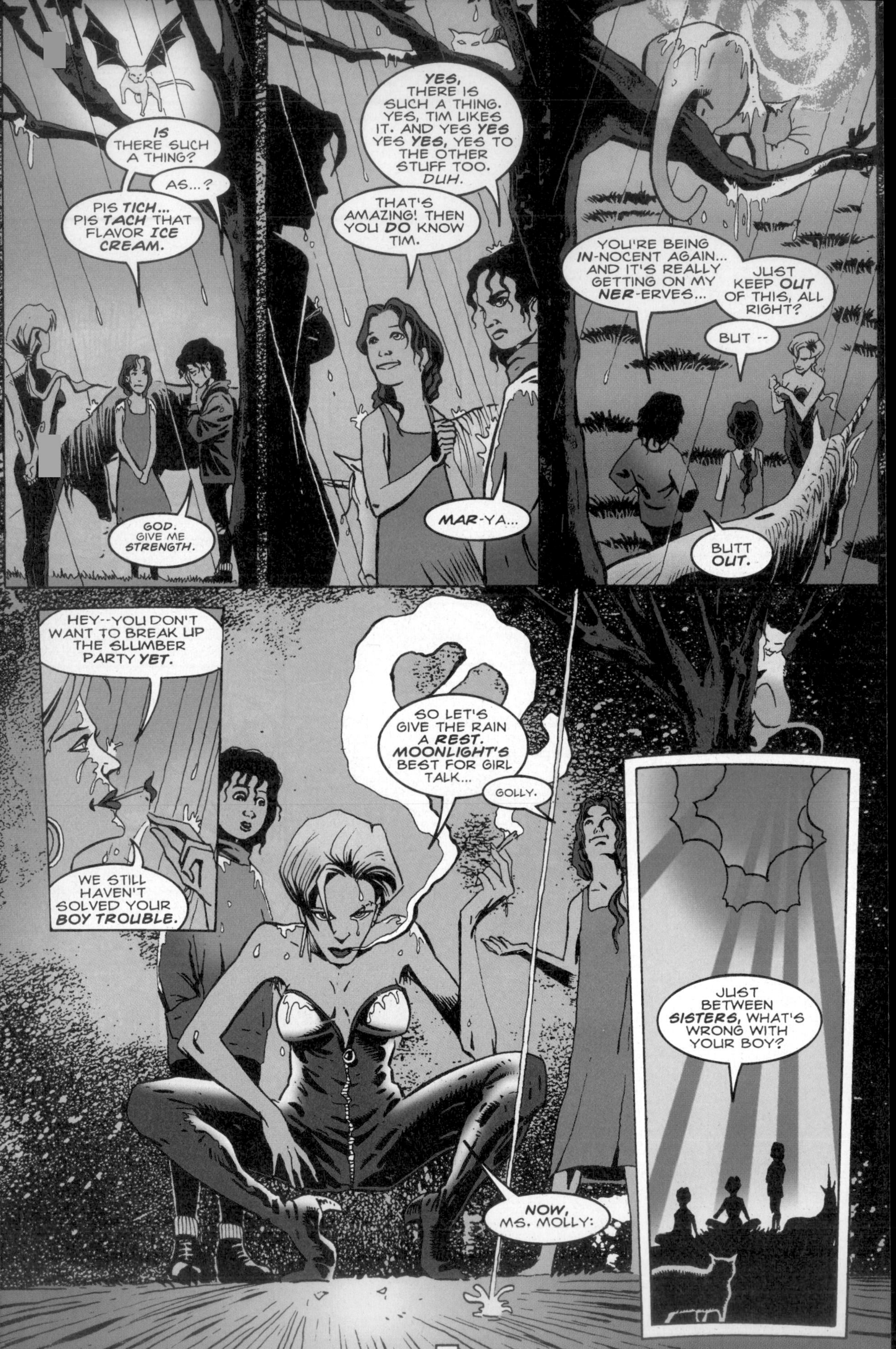
IS THERE SUCH A THING?
AS...?
PISTICH... PISTACH THAT FLAVOR ICE CREAM.
GOD. GIVE ME STRENGTH.
YES, THERE IS SUCH A THING. YES, TIM LIKES IT. AND YES YES YES YES, YES TO THE OTHER STUFF TOO. DUH.
THAT'S AMAZING! THEN YOU DO KNOW TIM.
MAR-YA...
YOU'RE BEING IN-NOCENT AGAIN... AND IT'S REALLY GETTING ON MY NER-ERVES...
JUST KEEP OUT OF THIS, ALL RIGHT?
BUT --
BUTT OUT.
HEY--YOU DON'T WANT TO BREAK UP THE SLUMBER PARTY YET.
WE STILL HAVEN'T SOLVED YOUR BOY TROUBLE.
SO LET'S GIVE THE RAIN A REST. MOONLIGHT'S BEST FOR GIRL TALK...
GOLLY.
NOW, MS. MOLLY:
JUST BETWEEN SISTERS, WHAT'S WRONG WITH YOUR BOY?

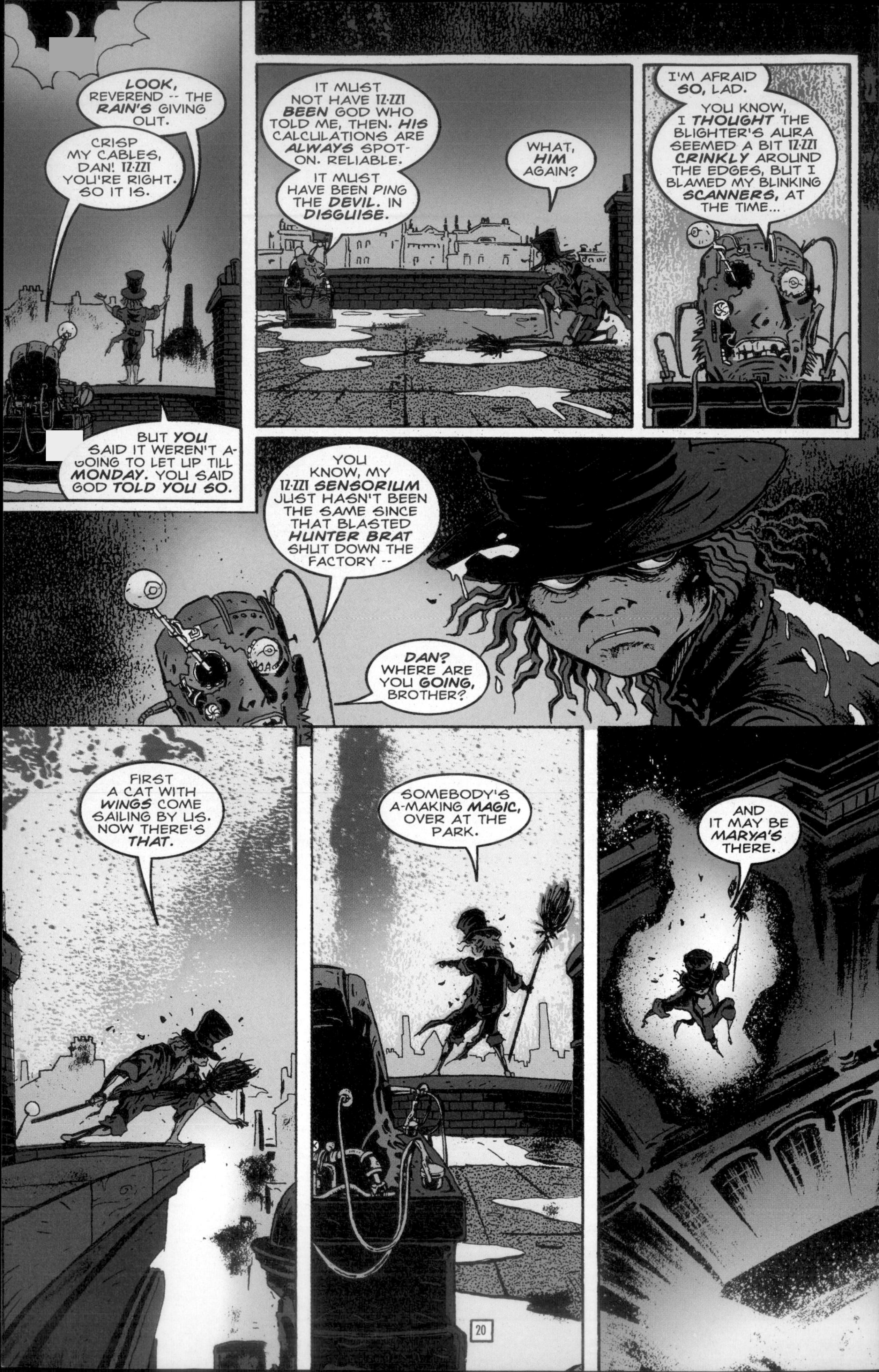
LOOK, REVEREND -- THE RAIN'S GIVING OUT.
CRISP MY CABLES, DAN! TZ-ZZT YOU'RE RIGHT. SO IT IS.
BUT YOU SAID IT WEREN'T A-GOING TO LET UP TILL MONDAY. YOU SAID GOD TOLD YOU SO.
IT MUST NOT HAVE TZ-ZZT BEEN GOD WHO TOLD ME, THEN. HIS CALCULATIONS ARE ALWAYS SPOT-ON. RELIABLE.
IT MUST HAVE BEEN PING THE DEVIL. IN DISGUISE.
WHAT, HIM AGAIN?
I'M AFRAID SO, LAD.
YOU KNOW, I THOUGHT THE BLIGHTER'S AURA SEEMED A BIT TZ-ZZT CRINKLY AROUND THE EDGES, BUT I BLAMED MY BLINKING SCANNERS, AT THE TIME...
YOU KNOW, MY TZ-ZZT SENSORIUM JUST HASN'T BEEN THE SAME SINCE THAT BLASTED HUNTER BRAT SHUT DOWN THE FACTORY --
DAN? WHERE ARE YOU GOING, BROTHER?
FIRST A CAT WITH WINGS COME SAILING BY US. NOW THERE'S THAT.
SOMEBODY'S A-MAKING MAGIC, OVER AT THE PARK.
AND IT MAY BE MARYA'S THERE.

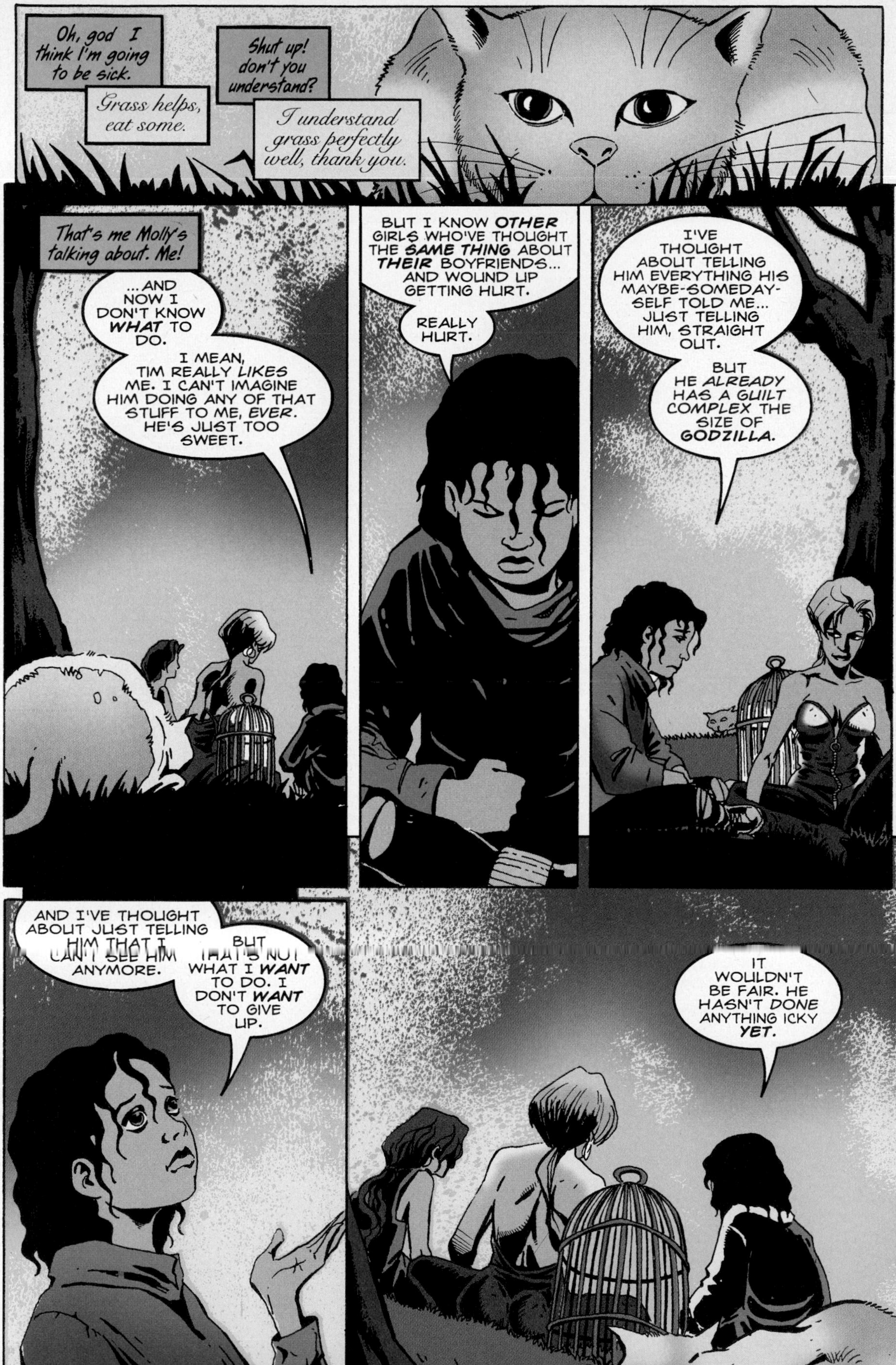
Oh, god I think I'm going to be sick.
Grass helps, eat some.
Shut up! don't you understand?
I understand grass perfectly well, thank you.
That's me Molly's talking about. Me!
...AND NOW I DON'T KNOW WHAT TO DO.
I MEAN, TIM REALLY LIKES ME. I CAN'T IMAGINE HIM DOING ANY OF THAT STUFF TO ME, EVER. HE'S JUST TOO SWEET.
BUT I KNOW OTHER GIRLS WHO'VE THOUGHT THE SAME THING ABOUT THEIR BOYFRIENDS... AND WOUND UP GETTING HURT.
REALLY HURT.
I'VE THOUGHT ABOUT TELLING HIM EVERYTHING HIS MAYBE-SOMEDAY-SELF TOLD ME... JUST TELLING HIM, STRAIGHT OUT.
BUT HE ALREADY HAS A GUILT COMPLEX THE SIZE OF GODZILLA.
AND I'VE THOUGHT ABOUT JUST TELLING HIM THAT I CAN'T SEE HIM ANYMORE.
BUT THAT'S NOT WHAT I WANT TO DO. I DON'T WANT TO GIVE UP.
IT WOULDN'T BE FAIR. HE HASN'T DONE ANYTHING ICKY YET.

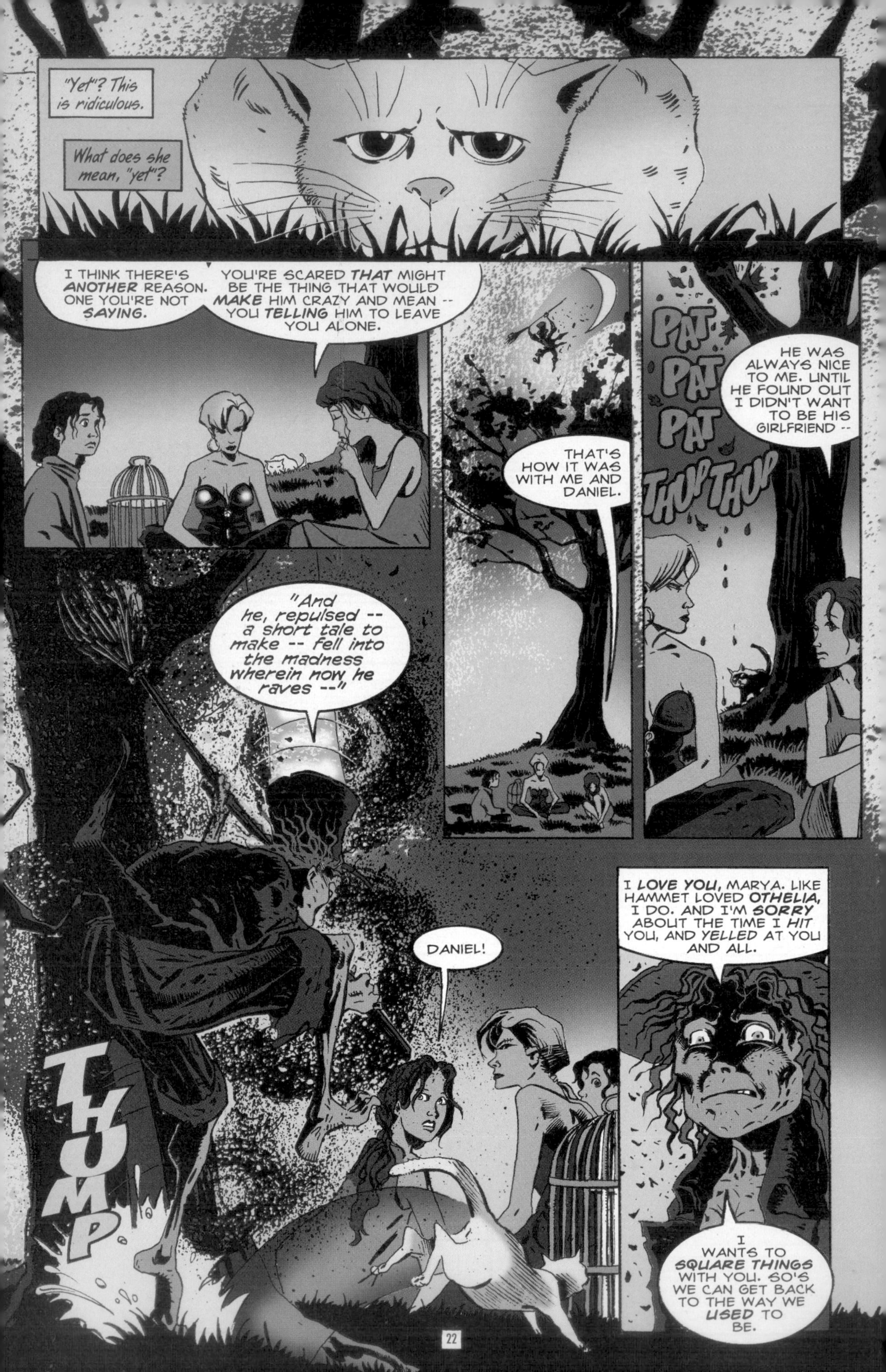
"Yet"? This is ridiculous.
What does she mean, "yet"?
I THINK THERE'S ANOTHER REASON. ONE YOU'RE NOT SAYING.
YOU'RE SCARED THAT MIGHT BE THE THING THAT WOULD MAKE HIM CRAZY AND MEAN -- YOU TELLING HIM TO LEAVE YOU ALONE.
THAT'S HOW IT WAS WITH ME AND DANIEL.
PAT PAT PAT
THUP THUP
HE WAS ALWAYS NICE TO ME. UNTIL HE FOUND OUT I DIDN'T WANT TO BE HIS GIRLFRIEND --
"And he, repulsed -- a short tale to make -- fell into the madness wherein now he raves --"
THUMP
DANIEL!
I LOVE YOU, MARYA. LIKE HAMMET LOVED OTHELIA, I DO. AND I'M SORRY ABOUT THE TIME I HIT YOU, AND YELLED AT YOU AND ALL.
I WANTS TO SQUARE THINGS WITH YOU. SO'S WE CAN GET BACK TO THE WAY WE USED TO BE.

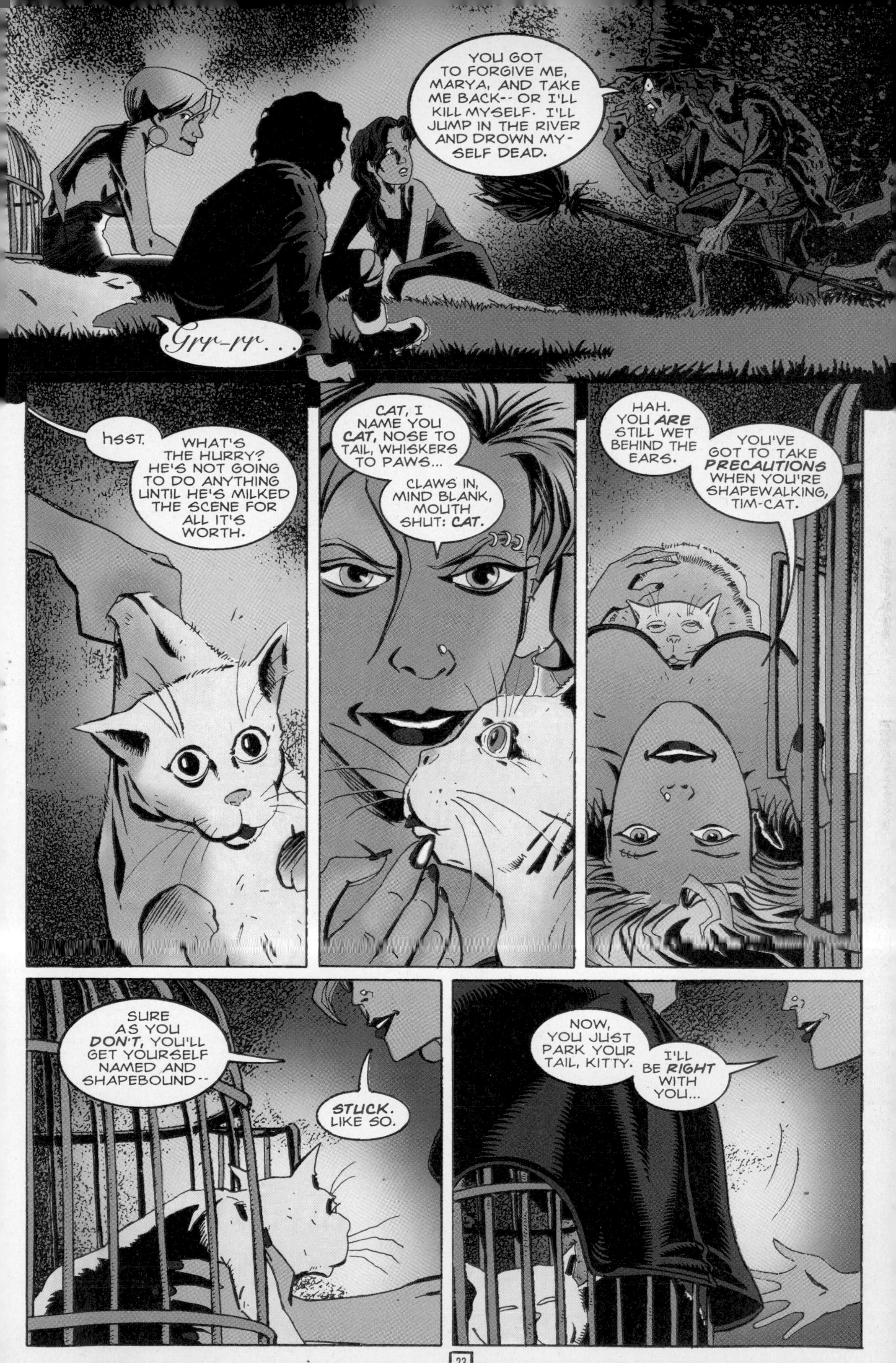

YOU GOT TO FORGIVE ME, MARYA, AND TAKE ME BACK-- OR I'LL KILL MYSELF. I'LL JUMP IN THE RIVER AND DROWN MY-SELF DEAD.
Grr-rr...
hsst.
WHAT'S THE HURRY? HE'S NOT GOING TO DO ANYTHING UNTIL HE'S MILKED THE SCENE FOR ALL IT'S WORTH.
CAT, I NAME YOU CAT, NOSE TO TAIL, WHISKERS TO PAWS...
CLAWS IN, MIND BLANK, MOUTH SHUT: CAT.
HAH. YOU ARE STILL WET BEHIND THE EARS.
YOU'VE GOT TO TAKE PRECAUTIONS WHEN YOU'RE SHAPEWALKING, TIM-CAT.
SURE AS YOU DON'T, YOU'LL GET YOURSELF NAMED AND SHAPEBOUND--
STUCK. LIKE SO.
NOW, YOU JUST PARK YOUR TAIL, KITTY.
I'LL BE RIGHT WITH YOU...

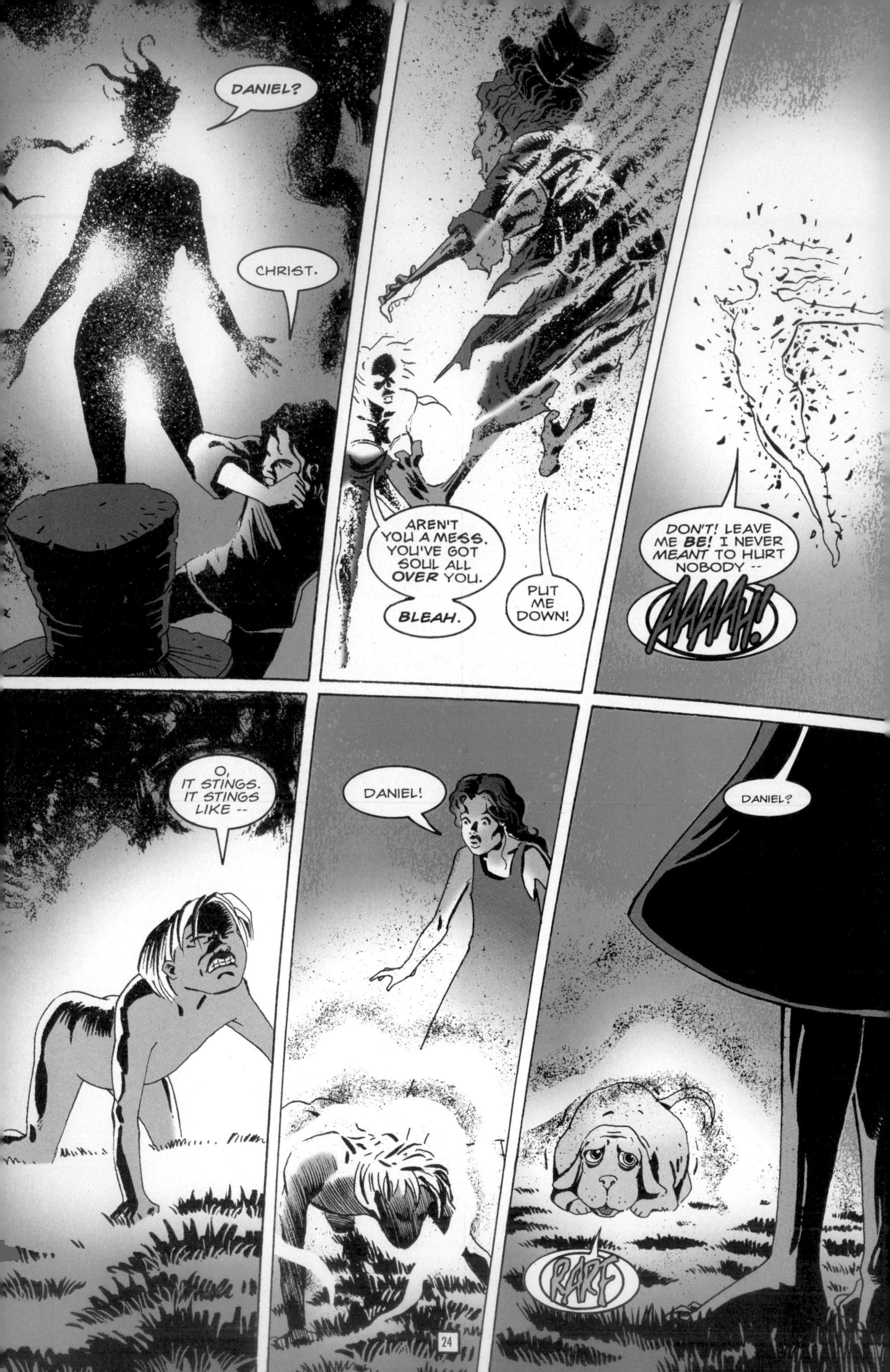
DANIEL?
CHRIST.
AREN'T YOU A MESS. YOU'VE GOT SOUL ALL OVER YOU.
BLEAH.
PUT ME DOWN!
DON'T! LEAVE ME BE! I NEVER MEANT TO HURT NOBODY --
AAAAH!
O, IT STINGS. IT STINGS LIKE --
DANIEL!
DANIEL?
RARF

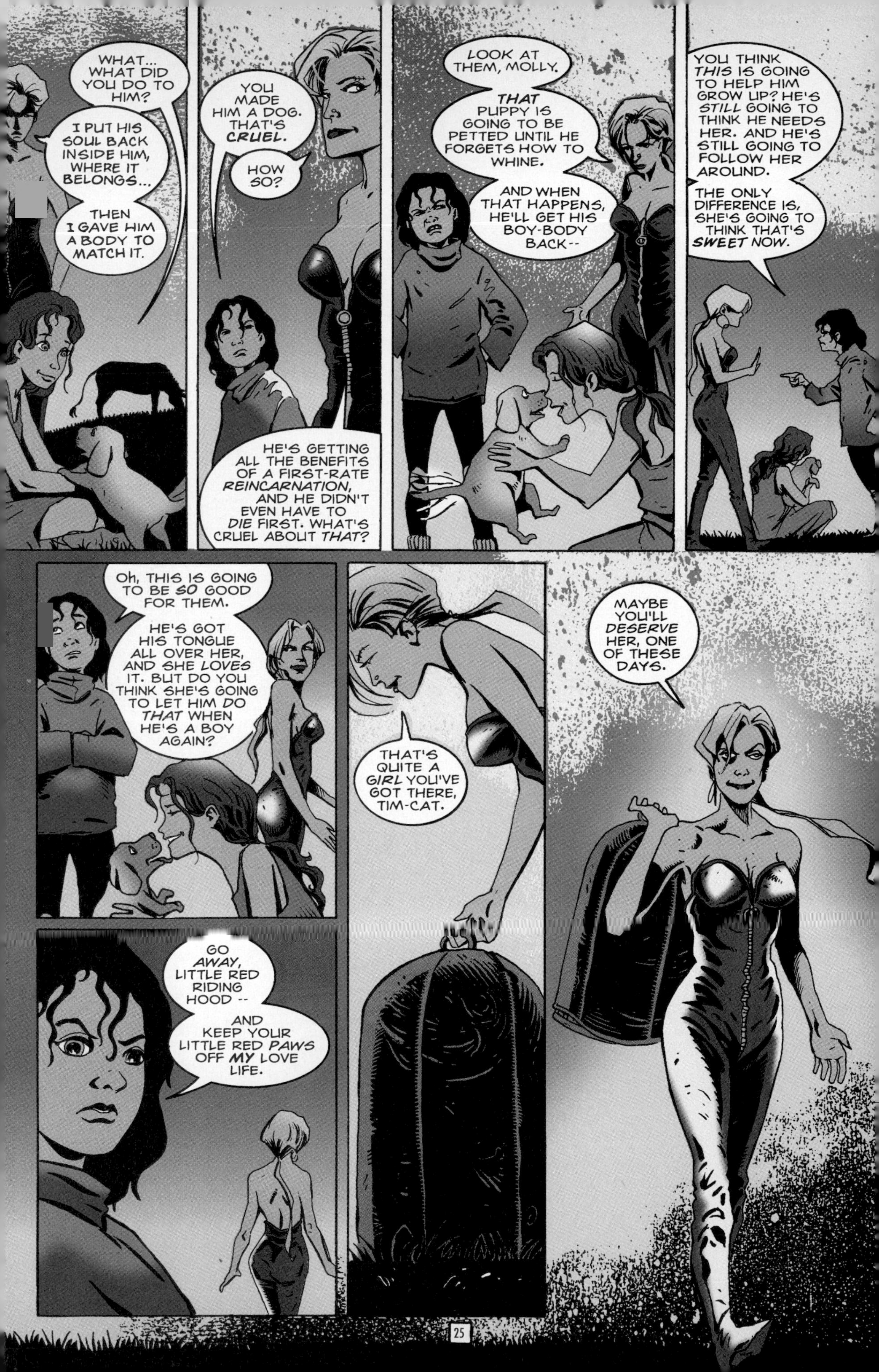

WHAT... WHAT DID YOU DO TO HIM?
I PUT HIS SOUL BACK INSIDE HIM, WHERE IT BELONGS...
THEN I GAVE HIM A BODY TO MATCH IT.
YOU MADE HIM A DOG. THAT'S CRUEL.
HOW SO?
HE'S GETTING ALL THE BENEFITS OF A FIRST-RATE REINCARNATION, AND HE DIDN'T EVEN HAVE TO DIE FIRST. WHAT'S CRUEL ABOUT THAT?
LOOK AT THEM, MOLLY.
THAT PUPPY IS GOING TO BE PETTED UNTIL HE FORGETS HOW TO WHINE.
AND WHEN THAT HAPPENS, HE'LL GET HIS BOY-BODY BACK--
YOU THINK THIS IS GOING TO HELP HIM GROW UP? HE'S STILL GOING TO THINK HE NEEDS HER. AND HE'S STILL GOING TO FOLLOW HER AROUND.
THE ONLY DIFFERENCE IS, SHE'S GOING TO THINK THAT'S SWEET NOW.
Oh, THIS IS GOING TO BE SO GOOD FOR THEM.
HE'S GOT HIS TONGUE ALL OVER HER, AND SHE LOVES IT. BUT DO YOU THINK SHE'S GOING TO LET HIM DO THAT WHEN HE'S A BOY AGAIN?
GO AWAY, LITTLE RED RIDING HOOD --
AND KEEP YOUR LITTLE RED PAWS OFF MY LOVE LIFE.
THAT'S QUITE A GIRL YOU'VE GOT THERE, TIM-CAT.
MAYBE YOU'LL DESERVE HER, ONE OF THESE DAYS.

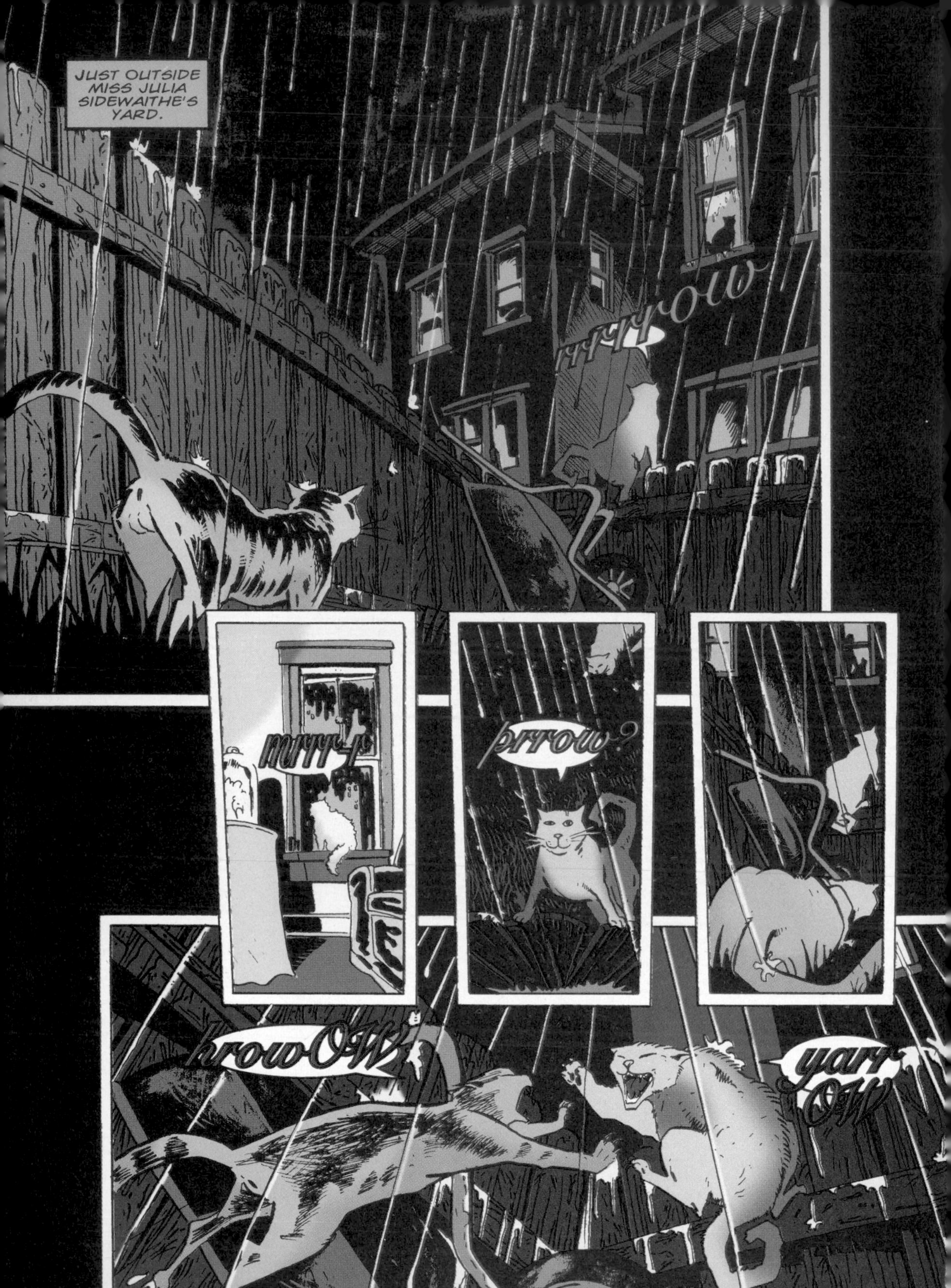
JUST OUTSIDE MISS JULIA SIDEWAITHE'S YARD.
rrrrrrOW
mrrr-r
prrow?
hrowOW
yarr OW

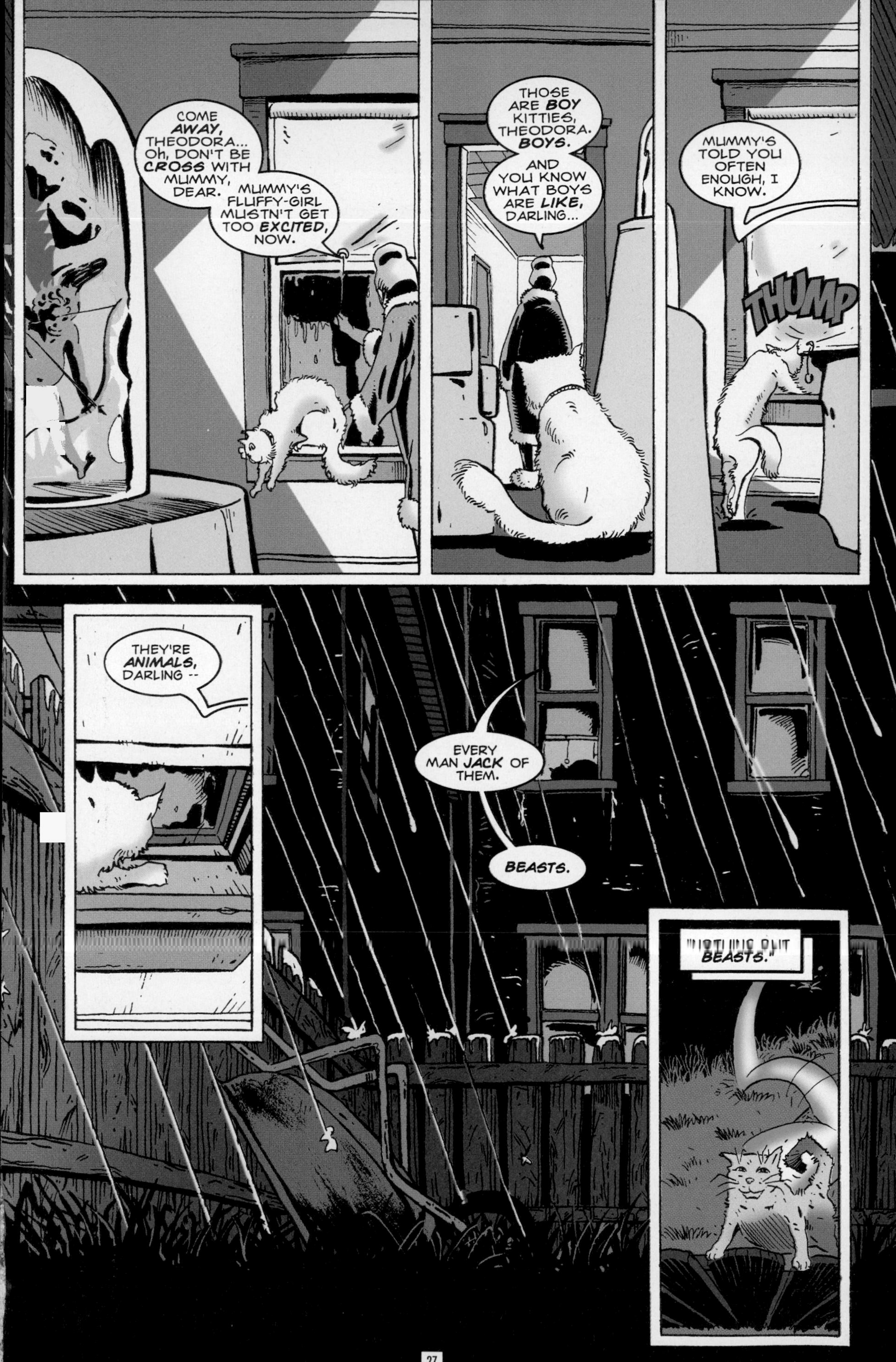
COME AWAY, THEODORA... Oh, DON'T BE CROSS WITH MUMMY, DEAR.
MUMMY'S FLUFFY-GIRL MUSTN'T GET TOO EXCITED, NOW.
THOSE ARE BOY KITTIES, THEODORA. BOYS.
AND YOU KNOW WHAT BOYS ARE LIKE, DARLING...
MUMMY'S TOLD YOU OFTEN ENOUGH, I KNOW.
THUMP
THEY'RE ANIMALS, DARLING --
EVERY MAN JACK OF THEM.
BEASTS.
BEASTS."

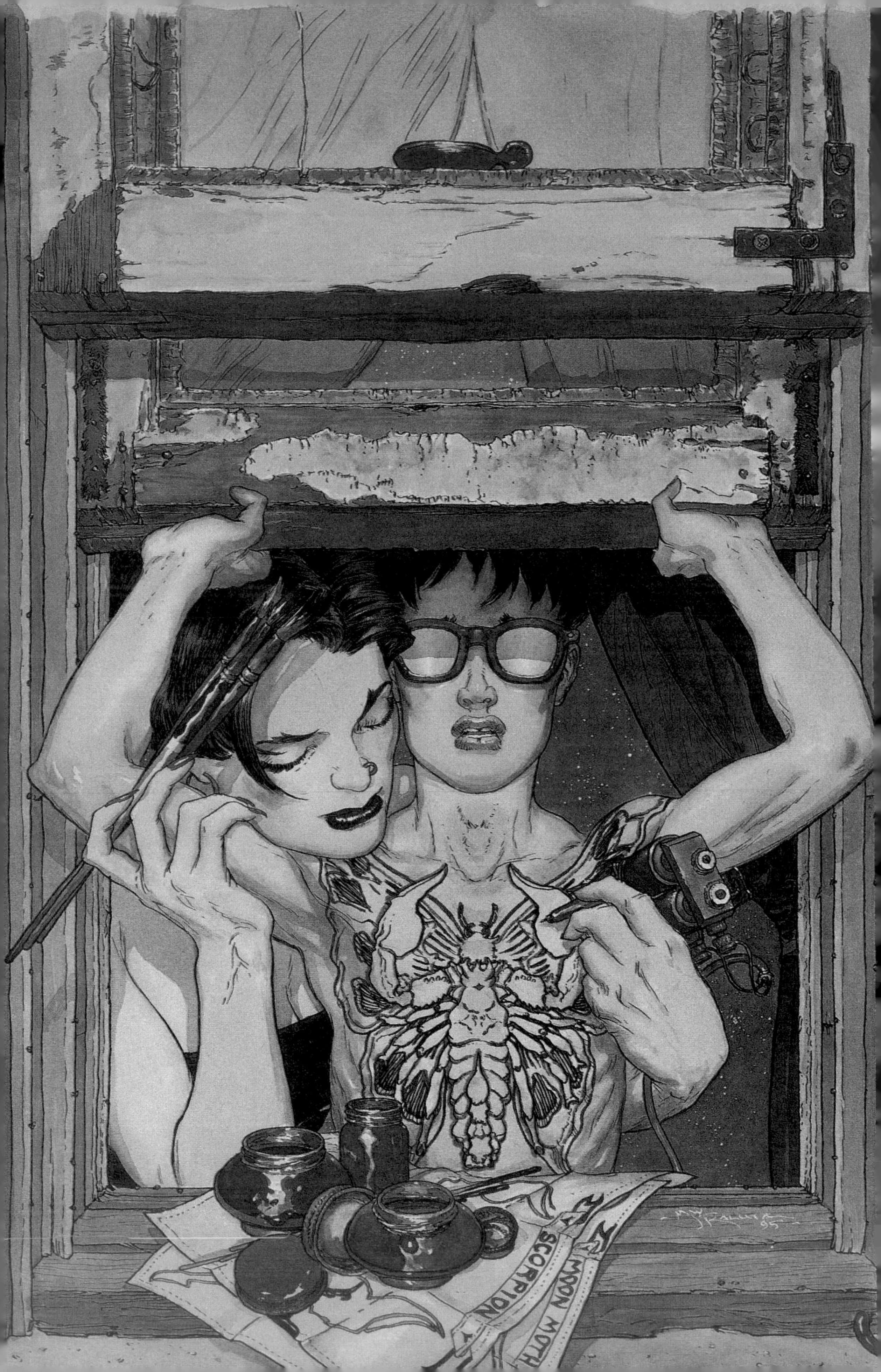
SCORPION
MOON MOTH

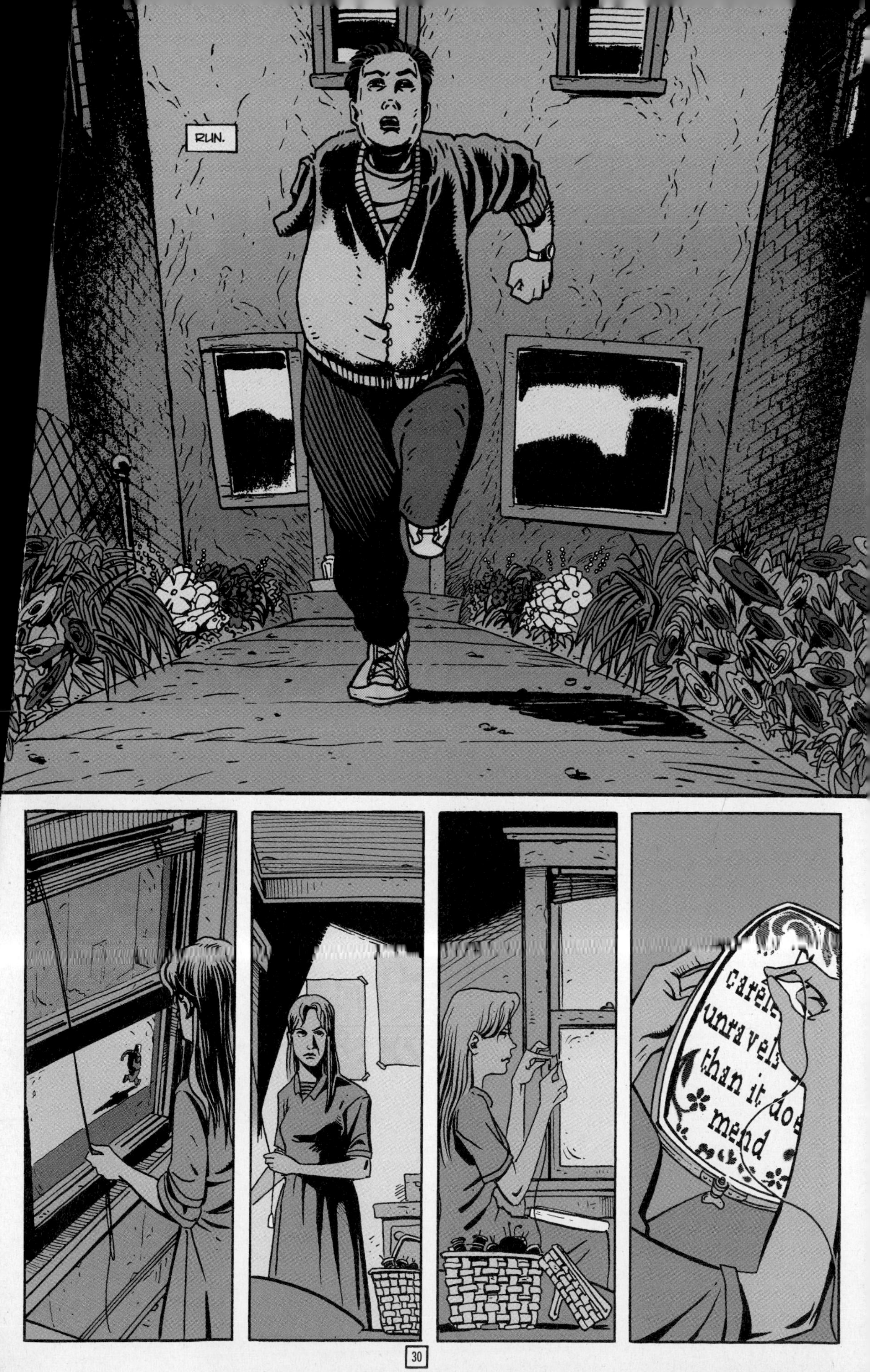
RUN.
carel
unravels
than it do
mend

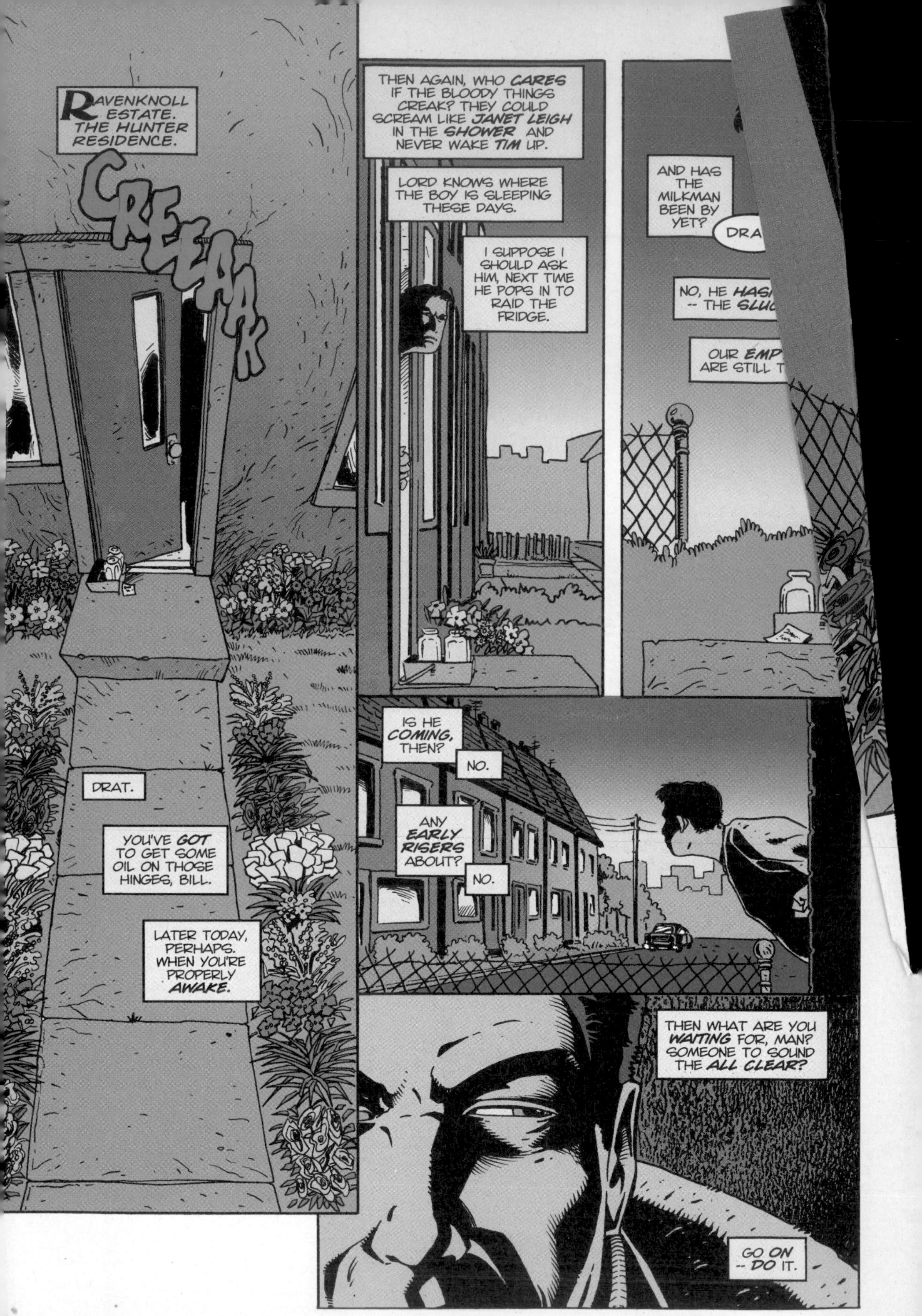
RAVENKNOLL ESTATE. THE HUNTER RESIDENCE.
CREEAAAK
DRAT.
YOU'VE GOT TO GET SOME OIL ON THOSE HINGES, BILL.
LATER TODAY, PERHAPS. WHEN YOU'RE PROPERLY AWAKE.
THEN AGAIN, WHO CARES IF THE BLOODY THINGS CREAK? THEY COULD SCREAM LIKE JANET LEIGH IN THE SHOWER AND NEVER WAKE TIM UP.
LORD KNOWS WHERE THE BOY IS SLEEPING THESE DAYS.
I SUPPOSE I SHOULD ASK HIM, NEXT TIME HE POPS IN TO RAID THE FRIDGE.
AND HAS THE MILKMAN BEEN BY YET?
IS HE COMING, THEN?
NO.
ANY EARLY RISERS ABOUT?
NO.
THEN WHAT ARE YOU WAITING FOR, MAN? SOMEONE TO SOUND THE ALL CLEAR?
GO ON -- DO IT.

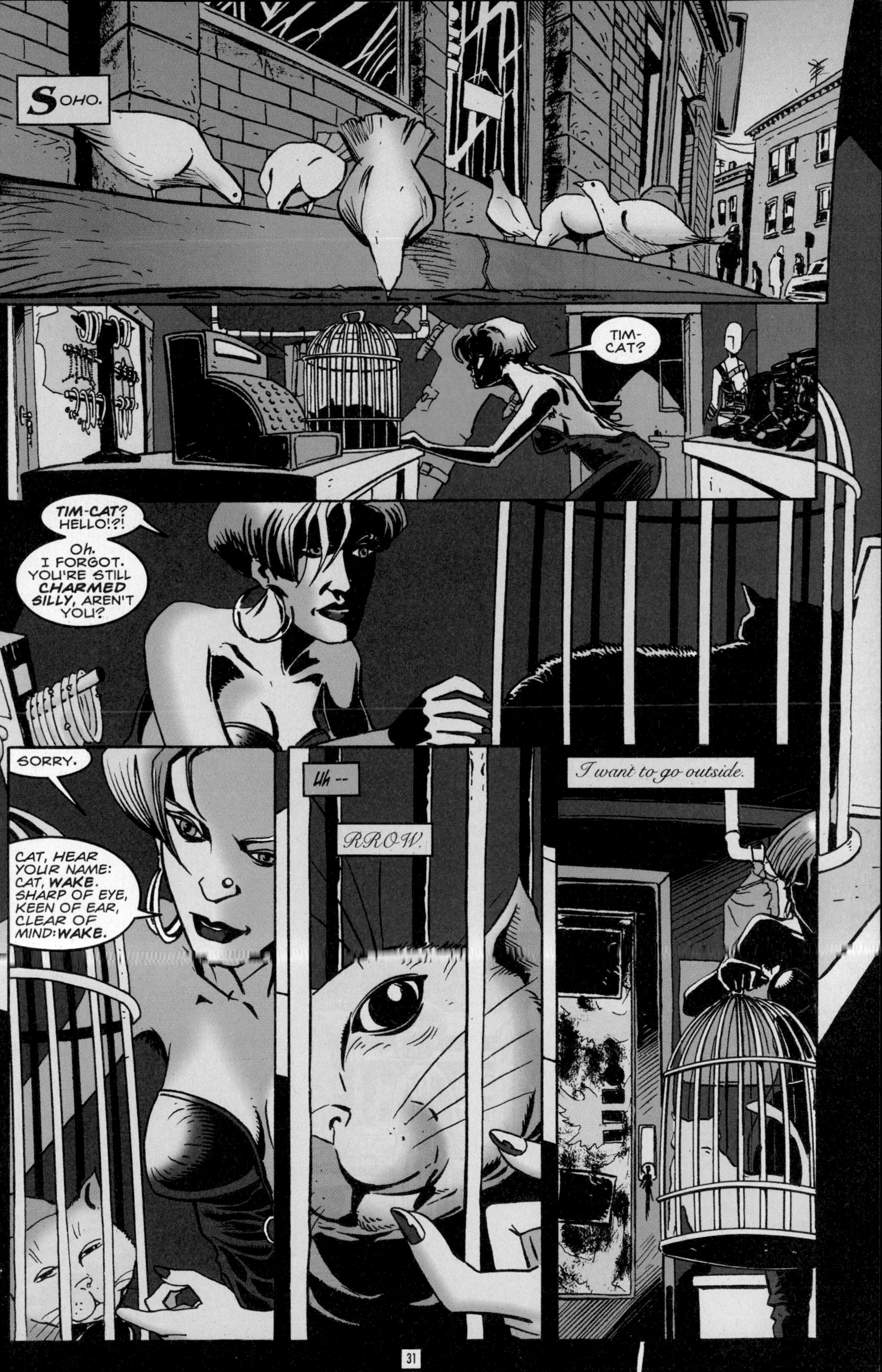
SOHO.
TIM-CAT?
TIM-CAT? HELLO!?!
Oh. I FORGOT. YOU'RE STILL CHARMED SILLY, AREN'T YOU?
SORRY.
CAT, HEAR YOUR NAME: CAT, WAKE. SHARP OF EYE, KEEN OF EAR, CLEAR OF MIND: WAKE.
Uh --
RROW.
I want to go outside.

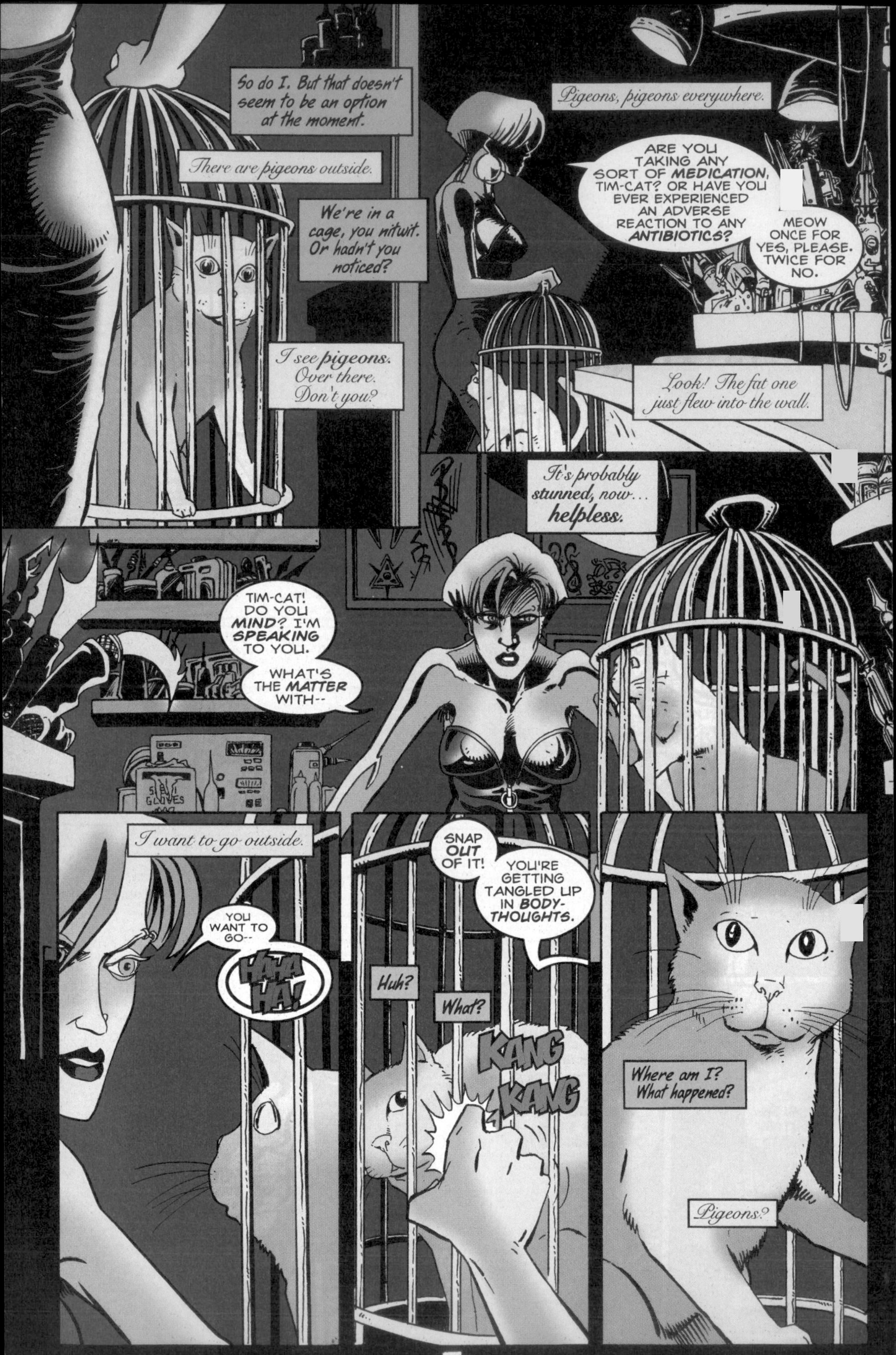

So do I. But that doesn't seem to be an option at the moment.
There are pigeons outside.
We're in a cage, you nitwit. Or hadn't you noticed?
I see pigeons. Over there. Don't you?
Pigeons, pigeons everywhere.
ARE YOU TAKING ANY SORT OF MEDICATION, TIM-CAT? OR HAVE YOU EVER EXPERIENCED AN ADVERSE REACTION TO ANY ANTIBIOTICS?
MEOW ONCE FOR YES, PLEASE. TWICE FOR NO.
Look! The fat one just flew into the wall.
It's probably stunned, now... helpless.
TIM-CAT! DO YOU MIND? I'M SPEAKING TO YOU.
WHAT'S THE MATTER WITH--
GLOVES
I want to go outside.
YOU WANT TO GO--
HAHA HA!
SNAP OUT OF IT!
YOU'RE GETTING TANGLED UP IN BODY-THOUGHTS.
Huh?
What?
KANG
KANG
Where am I? What happened?
Pigeons?

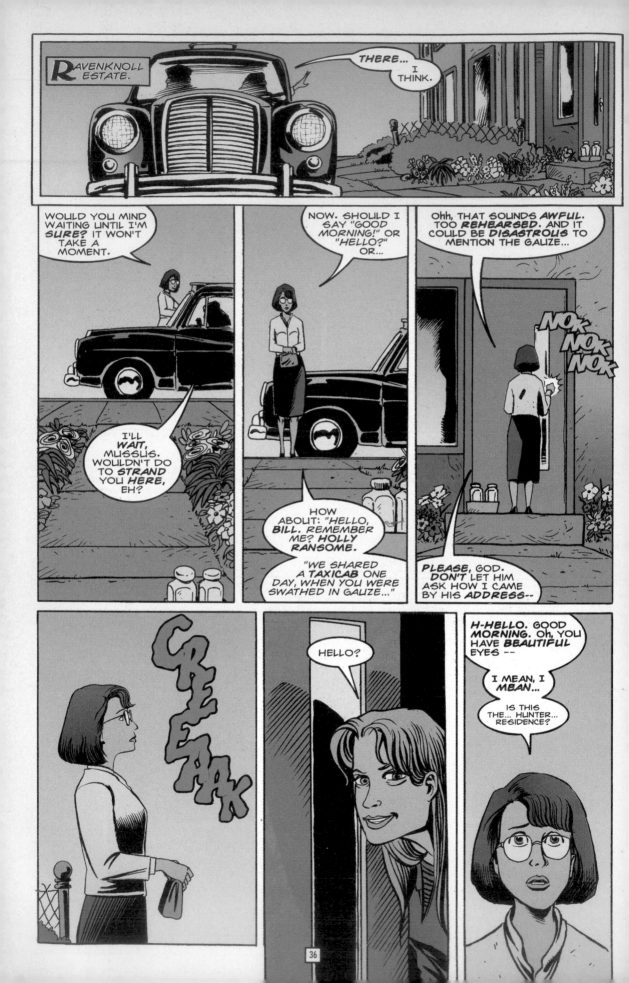

RAVENKNOLL ESTATE.

THERE... I THINK.

WOULD YOU MIND WAITING UNTIL I'M *SURE?* IT WON'T TAKE A MOMENT.

I'LL *WAIT,* MISSUS. WOULDN'T DO TO *STRAND* YOU *HERE,* EH?

NOW. SHOULD I SAY *"GOOD MORNING!"* OR *"HELLO?"* OR...

HOW ABOUT: *"HELLO, BILL. REMEMBER ME? HOLLY RANSOME.*

"WE SHARED A TAXICAB ONE DAY, WHEN YOU WERE SWATHED IN GAUZE..."

OHH, THAT SOUNDS *AWFUL.* TOO *REHEARSED.* AND IT COULD BE *DISASTROUS* TO MENTION THE GAUZE...

NOK NOK NOK

PLEASE, GOD. DON'T LET HIM ASK HOW I CAME BY HIS ADDRESS--

CREEAAK

HELLO?

H-HELLO. GOOD *MORNING.* OH, YOU HAVE *BEAUTIFUL* EYES --

I MEAN, I *MEAN...*

IS THIS THE... HUNTER... RESIDENCE?

36

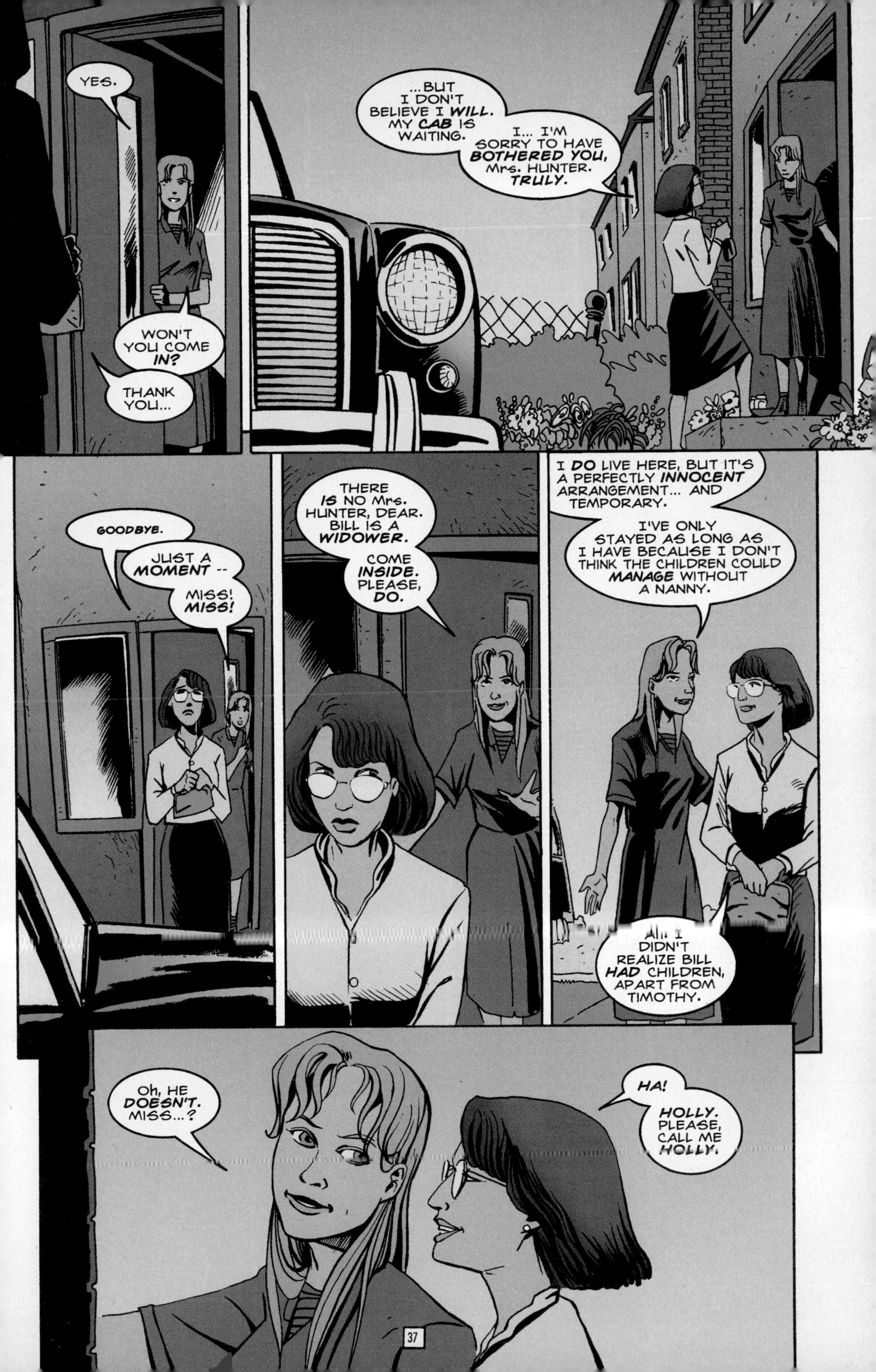
YES.
WON'T YOU COME ***IN?***
THANK YOU...
...BUT I DON'T BELIEVE I ***WILL.*** MY ***CAB*** IS WAITING.
I... I'M SORRY TO HAVE ***BOTHERED YOU,*** Mrs. HUNTER. ***TRULY.***
GOODBYE.
JUST A ***MOMENT*** --
MISS! ***MISS!***
THERE ***IS*** NO Mrs. HUNTER, DEAR. BILL IS A ***WIDOWER.***
COME ***INSIDE.*** PLEASE, ***DO.***
I ***DO*** LIVE HERE, BUT IT'S A PERFECTLY ***INNOCENT*** ARRANGEMENT... AND TEMPORARY.
I'VE ONLY STAYED AS LONG AS I HAVE BECAUSE I DON'T THINK THE CHILDREN COULD ***MANAGE*** WITHOUT A NANNY.
I DIDN'T REALIZE BILL ***HAD*** CHILDREN, APART FROM TIMOTHY.
Oh, HE ***DOESN'T.*** MISS...?
HA!
HOLLY. PLEASE, CALL ME ***HOLLY.***

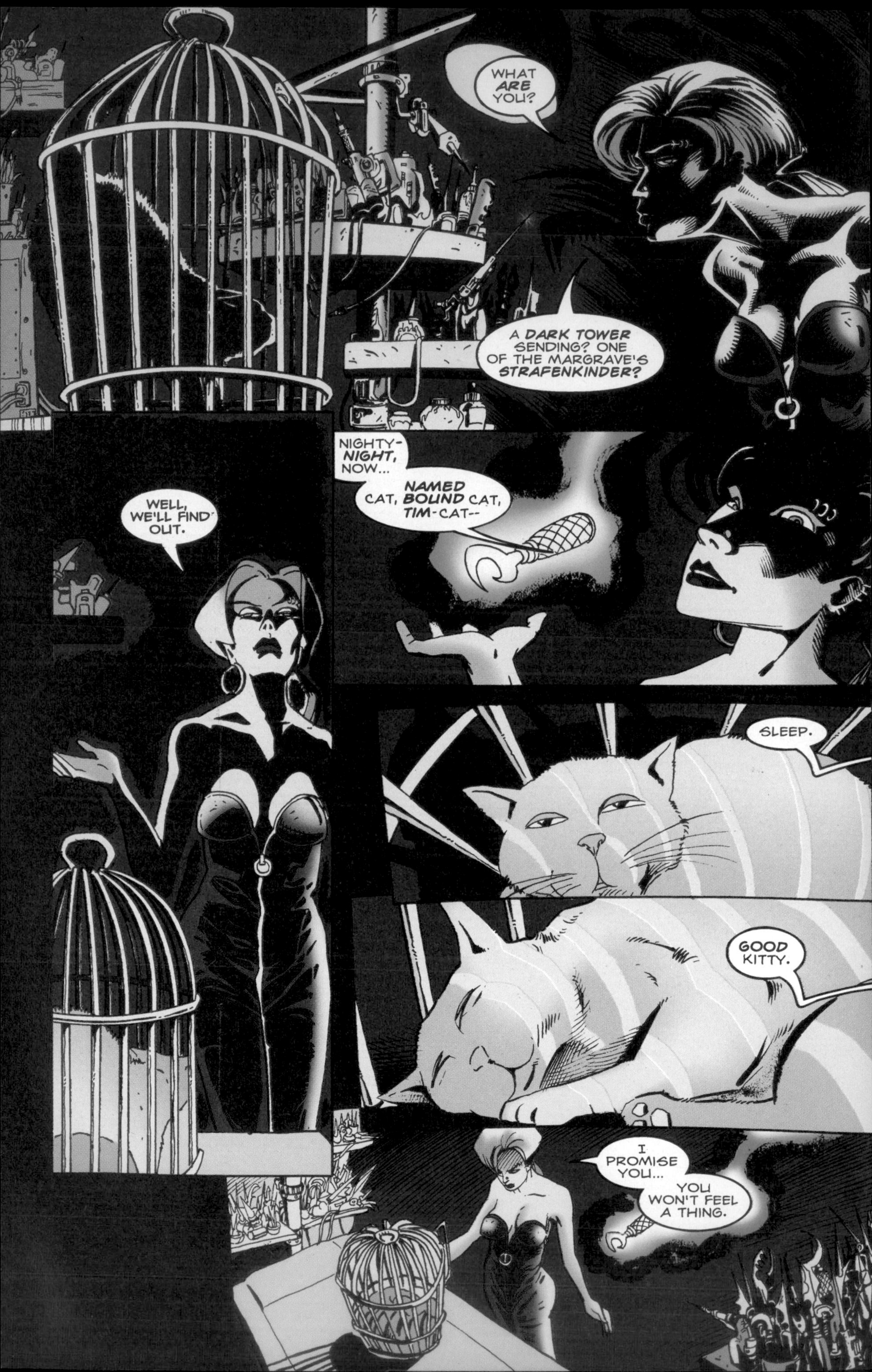
WHAT ARE YOU?
A DARK TOWER SENDING? ONE OF THE MARGRAVE'S STRAFENKINDER?
WELL, WE'LL FIND OUT.
NIGHTY-NIGHT, NOW...
NAMED CAT, BOUND CAT, TIM-CAT--
SLEEP.
GOOD KITTY.
I PROMISE YOU...
YOU WON'T FEEL A THING.

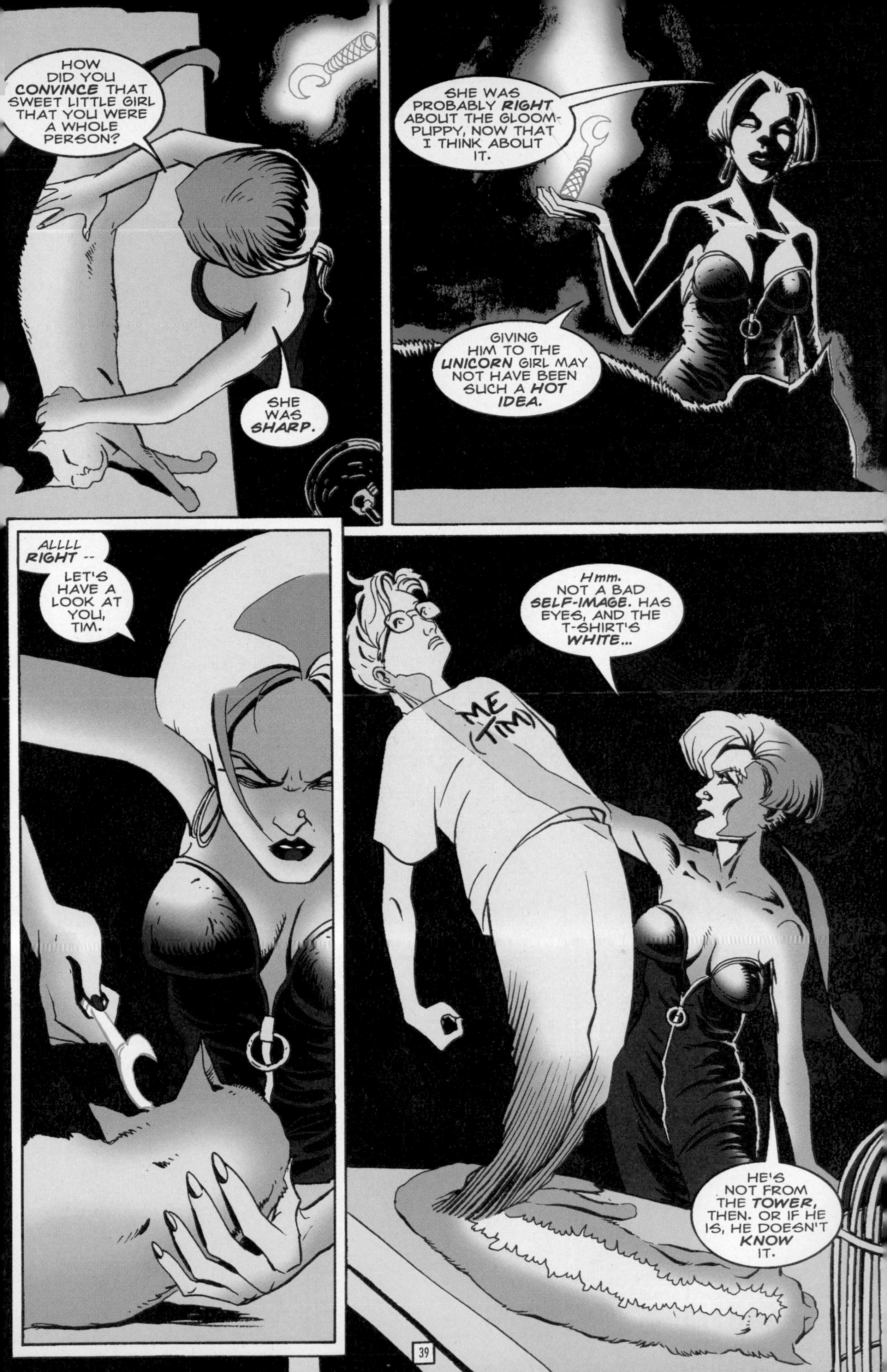
HOW DID YOU CONVINCE THAT SWEET LITTLE GIRL THAT YOU WERE A WHOLE PERSON?
SHE WAS SHARP.
SHE WAS PROBABLY RIGHT ABOUT THE GLOOM-PUPPY, NOW THAT I THINK ABOUT IT.
GIVING HIM TO THE UNICORN GIRL MAY NOT HAVE BEEN SUCH A HOT IDEA.
ALLLL RIGHT -- LET'S HAVE A LOOK AT YOU, TIM.
Hmm. NOT A BAD SELF-IMAGE. HAS EYES, AND THE T-SHIRT'S WHITE...
ME (TIM)
HE'S NOT FROM THE TOWER, THEN. OR IF HE IS, HE DOESN'T KNOW IT.

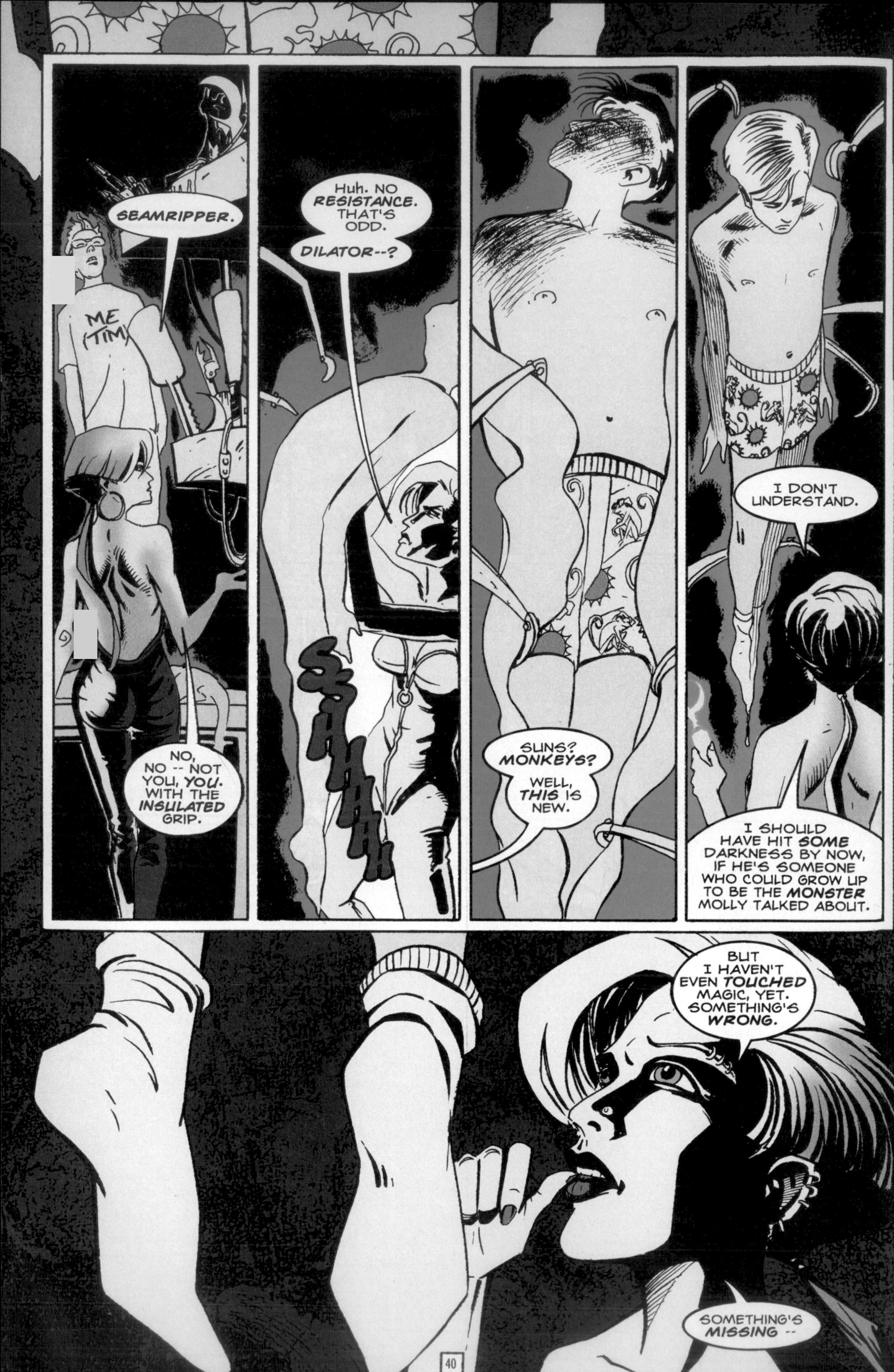
SEAMRIPPER.
ME (TIM)
NO, NO -- NOT YOU, YOU. WITH THE INSULATED GRIP.
Huh. NO RESISTANCE. THAT'S ODD.
DILATOR--?
SSHHHHH
SUNS? MONKEYS?
WELL, THIS IS NEW.
I DON'T UNDERSTAND.
I SHOULD HAVE HIT SOME DARKNESS BY NOW, IF HE'S SOMEONE WHO COULD GROW UP TO BE THE MONSTER MOLLY TALKED ABOUT.
BUT I HAVEN'T EVEN TOUCHED MAGIC, YET. SOMETHING'S WRONG.
SOMETHING'S MISSING --

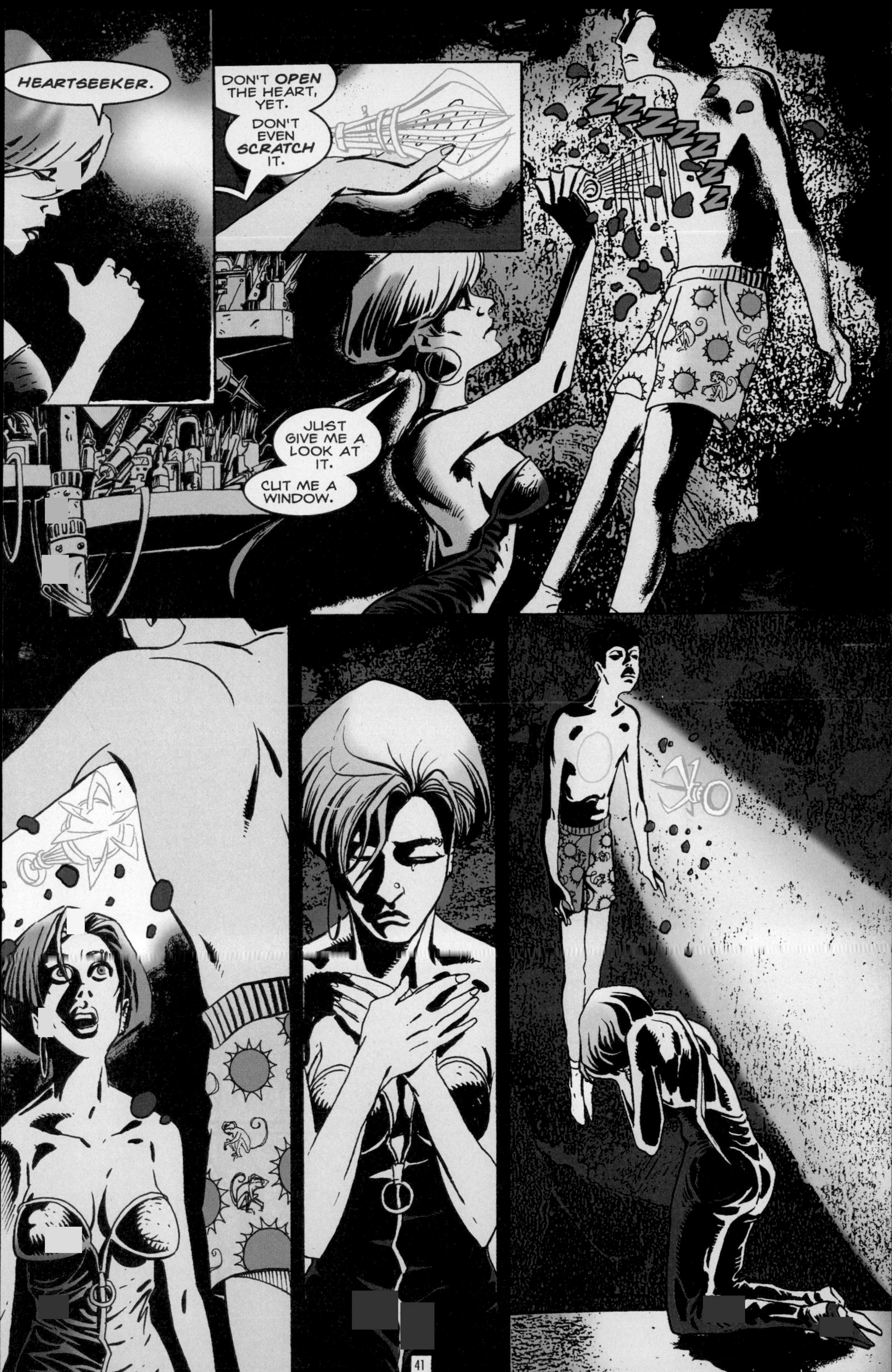
HEARTSEEKER.
DON'T OPEN THE HEART, YET.
DON'T EVEN SCRATCH IT.
JUST GIVE ME A LOOK AT IT.
CUT ME A WINDOW.

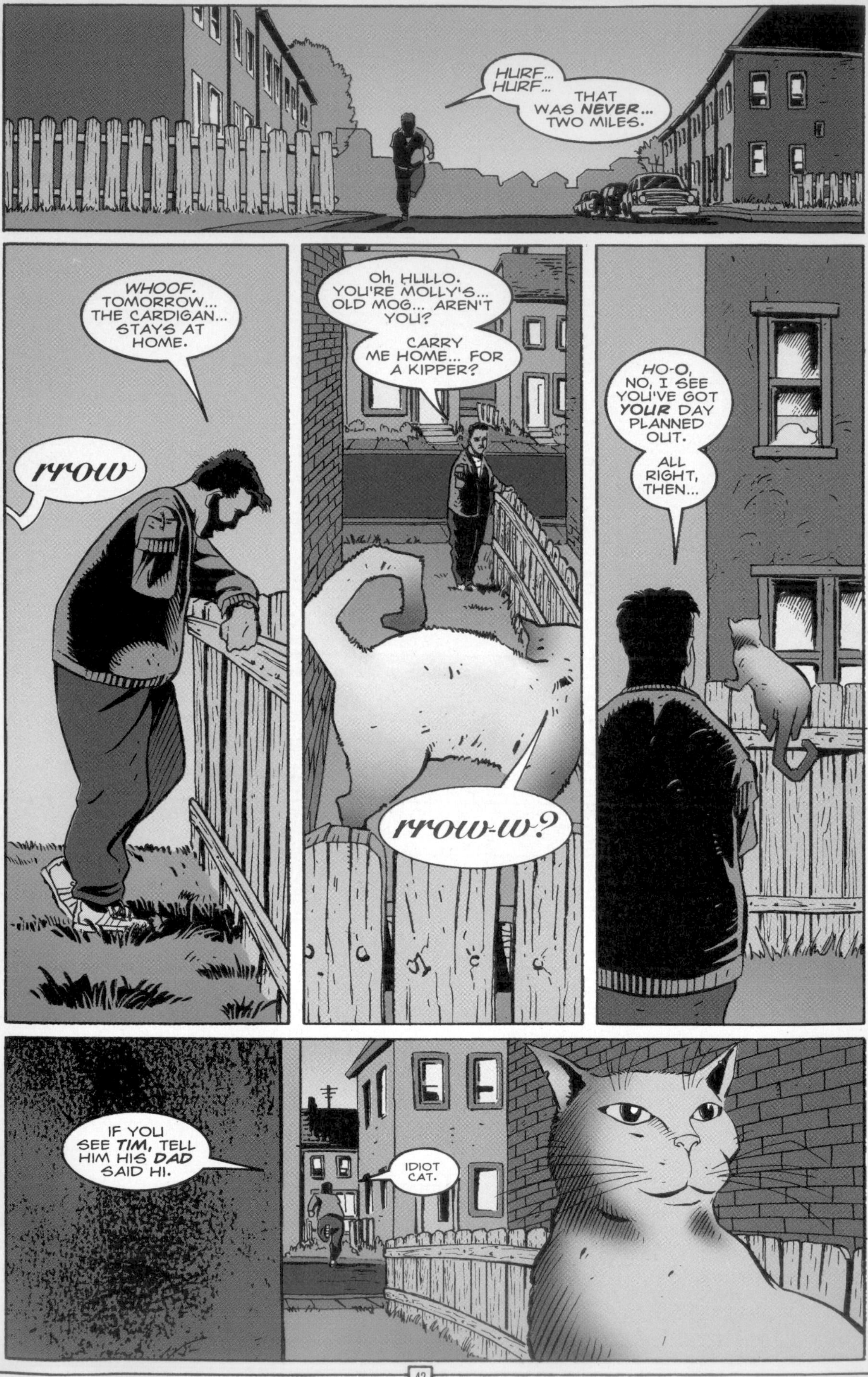
HURF... HURF... THAT WAS NEVER... TWO MILES.
WHOOF. TOMORROW... THE CARDIGAN... STAYS AT HOME.
rrow
Oh, HULLO. YOU'RE MOLLY'S... OLD MOG... AREN'T YOU?
CARRY ME HOME... FOR A KIPPER?
rrow-w?
HO-O, NO, I SEE YOU'VE GOT YOUR DAY PLANNED OUT.
ALL RIGHT, THEN...
IF YOU SEE TIM, TELL HIM HIS DAD SAID HI.
IDIOT CAT.

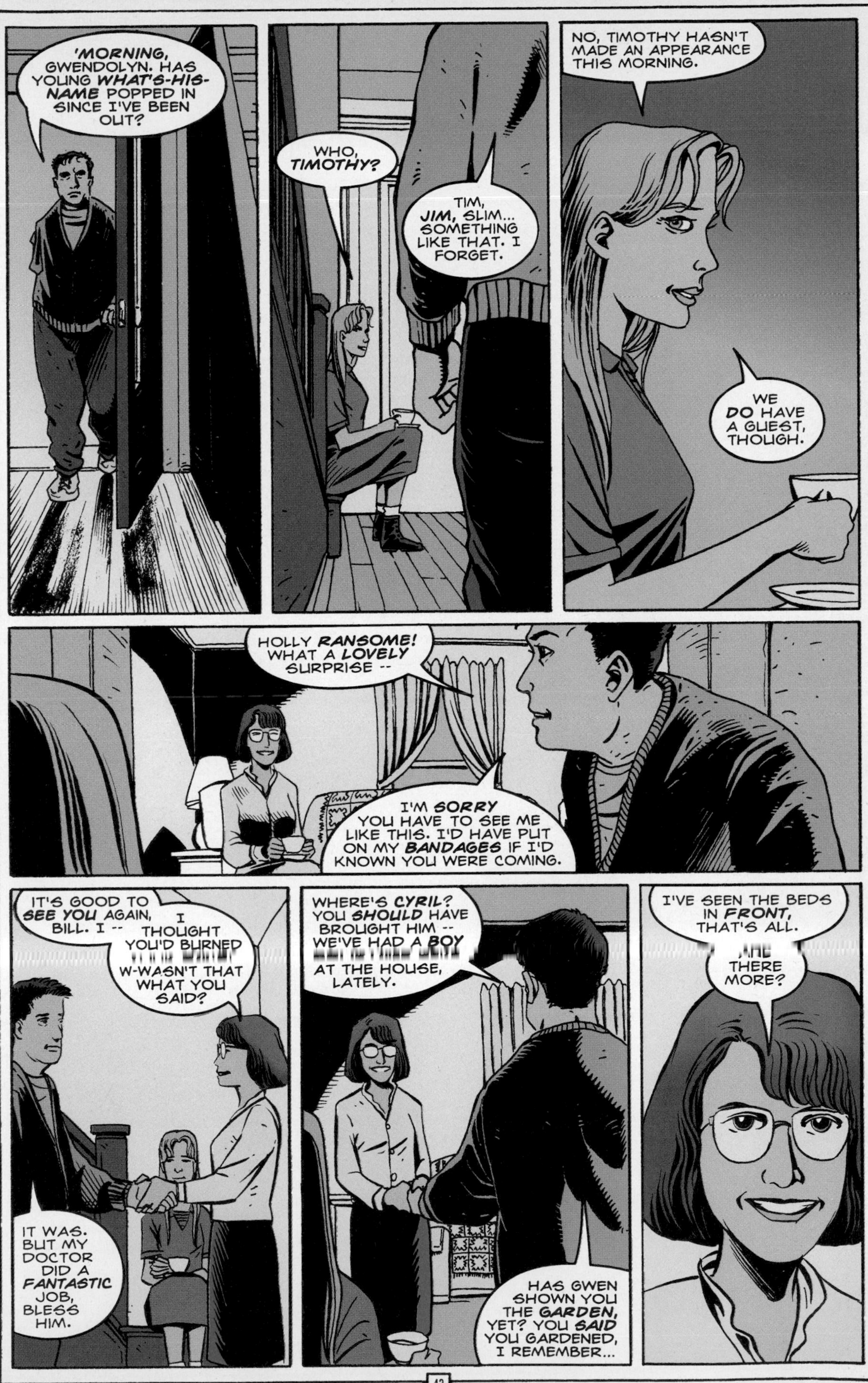
'MORNING, GWENDOLYN. HAS YOUNG WHAT'S-HIS-NAME POPPED IN SINCE I'VE BEEN OUT?
WHO, TIMOTHY?
TIM, JIM, SLIM... SOMETHING LIKE THAT. I FORGET.
NO, TIMOTHY HASN'T MADE AN APPEARANCE THIS MORNING.
WE DO HAVE A GUEST, THOUGH.
HOLLY RANSOME! WHAT A LOVELY SURPRISE --
I'M SORRY YOU HAVE TO SEE ME LIKE THIS. I'D HAVE PUT ON MY BANDAGES IF I'D KNOWN YOU WERE COMING.
IT'S GOOD TO SEE YOU AGAIN, BILL. I --
I THOUGHT YOU'D BURNED
W-WASN'T THAT WHAT YOU SAID?
IT WAS. BUT MY DOCTOR DID A FANTASTIC JOB, BLESS HIM.
WHERE'S CYRIL? YOU SHOULD HAVE BROUGHT HIM -- WE'VE HAD A BOY
AT THE HOUSE, LATELY.
HAS GWEN SHOWN YOU THE GARDEN, YET? YOU SAID YOU GARDENED, I REMEMBER...
I'VE SEEN THE BEDS IN FRONT, THAT'S ALL.
THERE MORE?

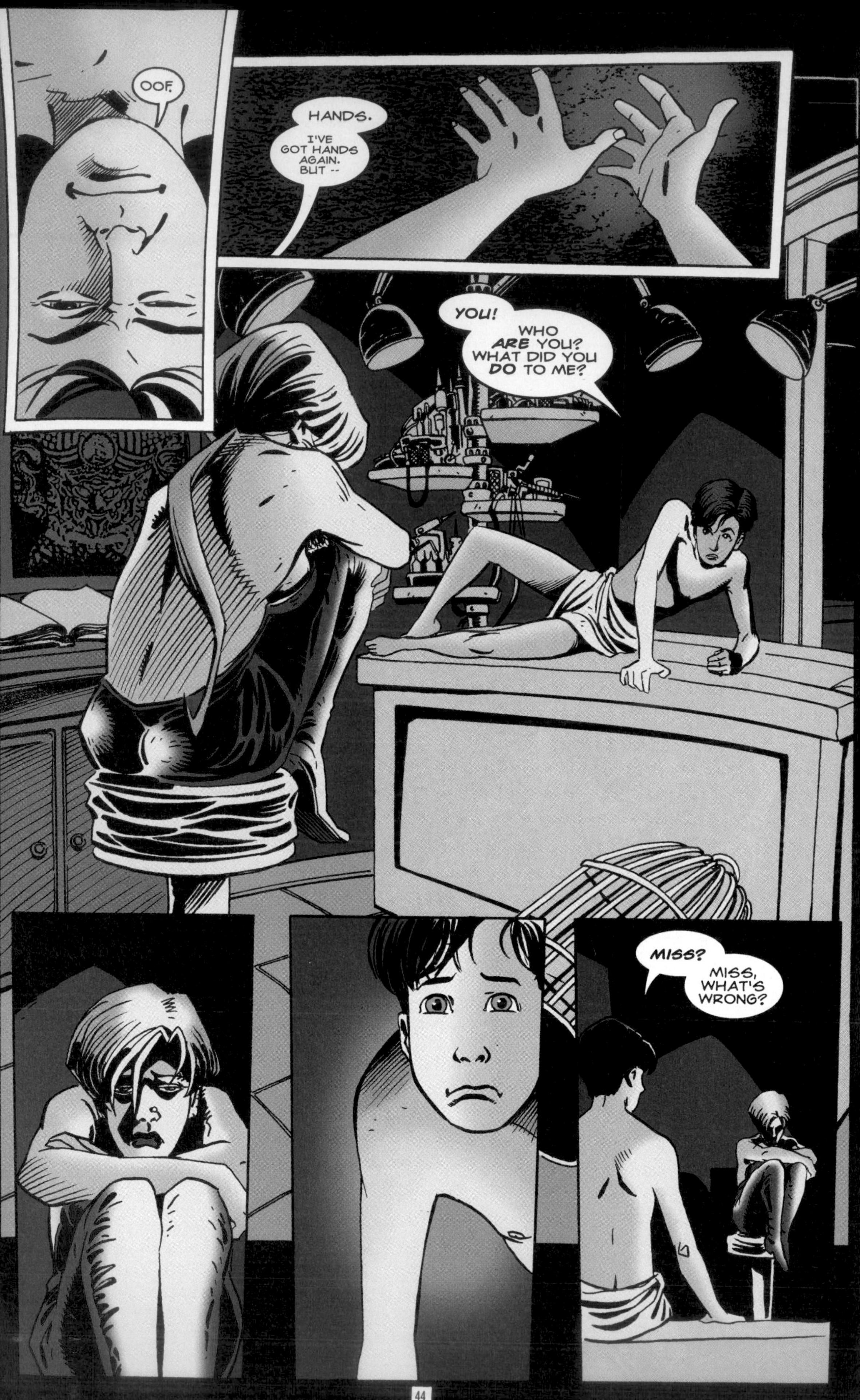
OOF.
HANDS.
I'VE GOT HANDS AGAIN. BUT --
YOU! WHO ARE YOU? WHAT DID YOU DO TO ME?
MISS?
MISS, WHAT'S WRONG?

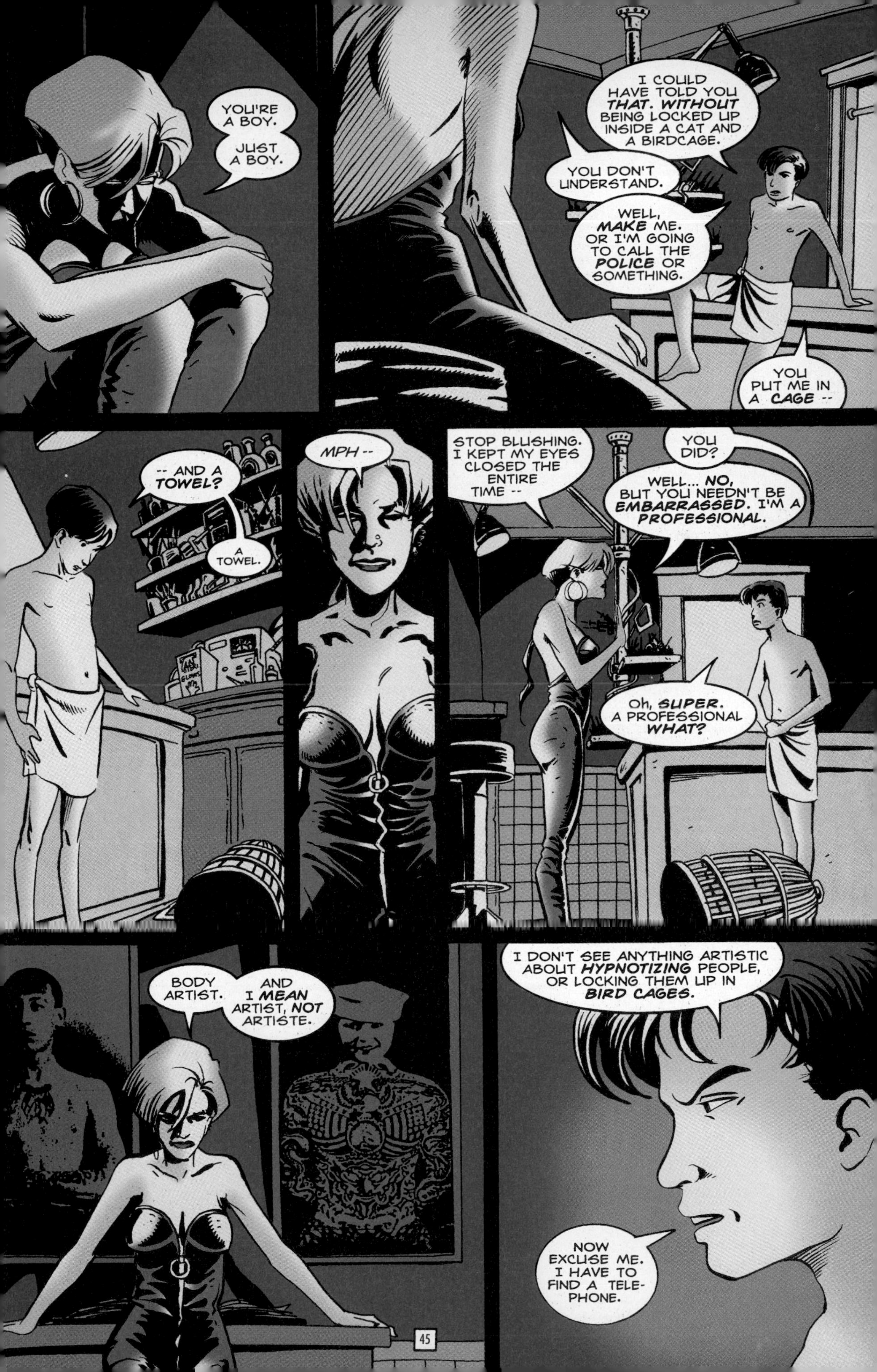

YOU'RE A BOY.
JUST A BOY.
I COULD HAVE TOLD YOU THAT. WITHOUT BEING LOCKED UP INSIDE A CAT AND A BIRDCAGE.
YOU DON'T UNDERSTAND.
WELL, MAKE ME. OR I'M GOING TO CALL THE POLICE OR SOMETHING.
YOU PUT ME IN A CAGE --
-- AND A TOWEL?
A TOWEL.
MPH --
STOP BLUSHING. I KEPT MY EYES CLOSED THE ENTIRE TIME --
YOU DID?
WELL... NO, BUT YOU NEEDN'T BE EMBARRASSED. I'M A PROFESSIONAL.
Oh, SUPER. A PROFESSIONAL WHAT?
BODY ARTIST.
AND I MEAN ARTIST, NOT ARTISTE.
I DON'T SEE ANYTHING ARTISTIC ABOUT HYPNOTIZING PEOPLE, OR LOCKING THEM UP IN BIRD CAGES.
NOW EXCUSE ME. I HAVE TO FIND A TELE-PHONE.

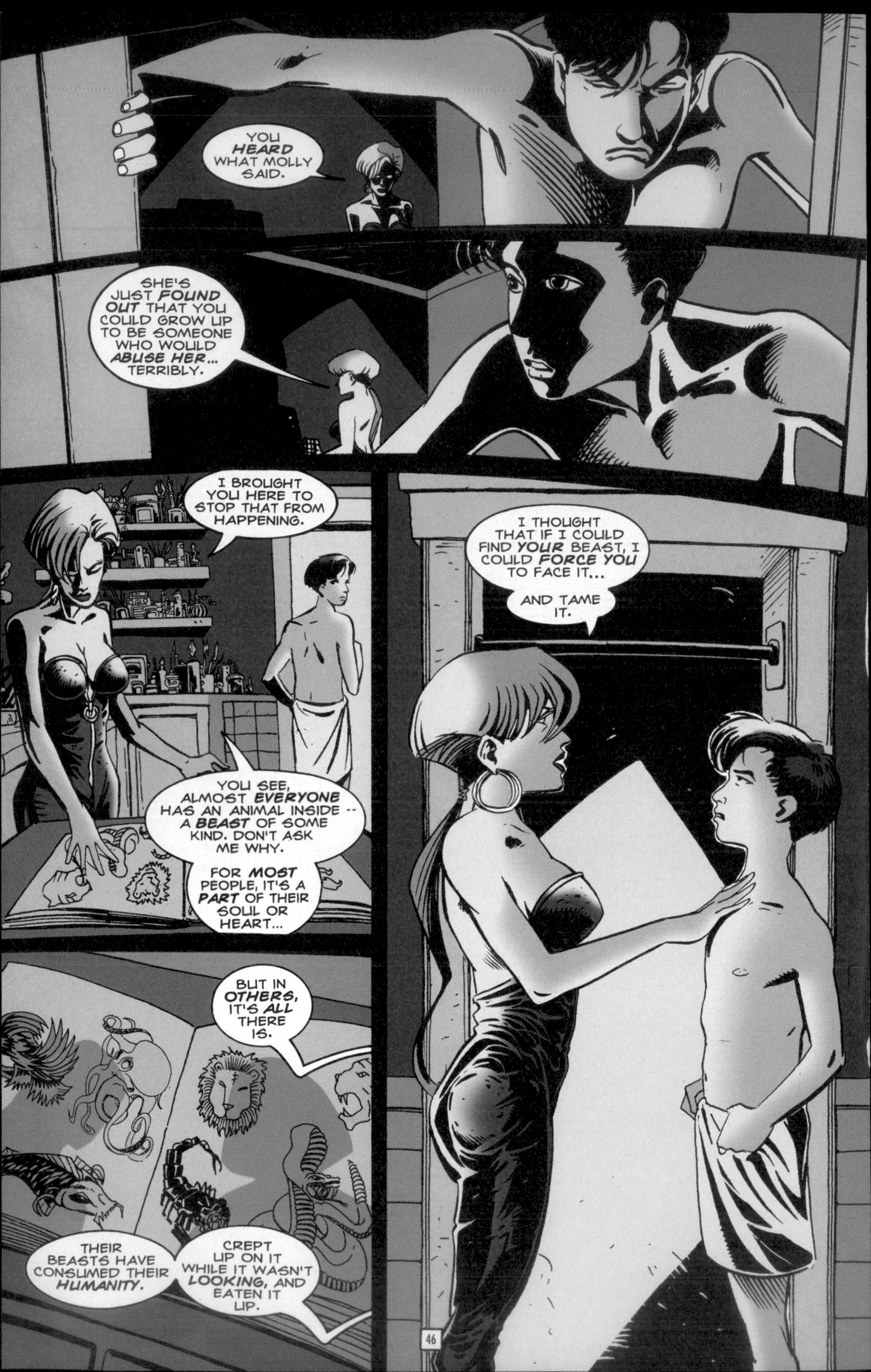
YOU HEARD WHAT MOLLY SAID.
SHE'S JUST FOUND OUT THAT YOU COULD GROW UP TO BE SOMEONE WHO WOULD ABUSE HER... TERRIBLY.
I BROUGHT YOU HERE TO STOP THAT FROM HAPPENING.
YOU SEE, ALMOST EVERYONE HAS AN ANIMAL INSIDE -- A BEAST OF SOME KIND. DON'T ASK ME WHY.
FOR MOST PEOPLE, IT'S A PART OF THEIR SOUL OR HEART...
BUT IN OTHERS, IT'S ALL THERE IS.
THEIR BEASTS HAVE CONSUMED THEIR HUMANITY.
CREPT UP ON IT WHILE IT WASN'T LOOKING, AND EATEN IT UP.
I THOUGHT THAT IF I COULD FIND YOUR BEAST, I COULD FORCE YOU TO FACE IT...
AND TAME IT.

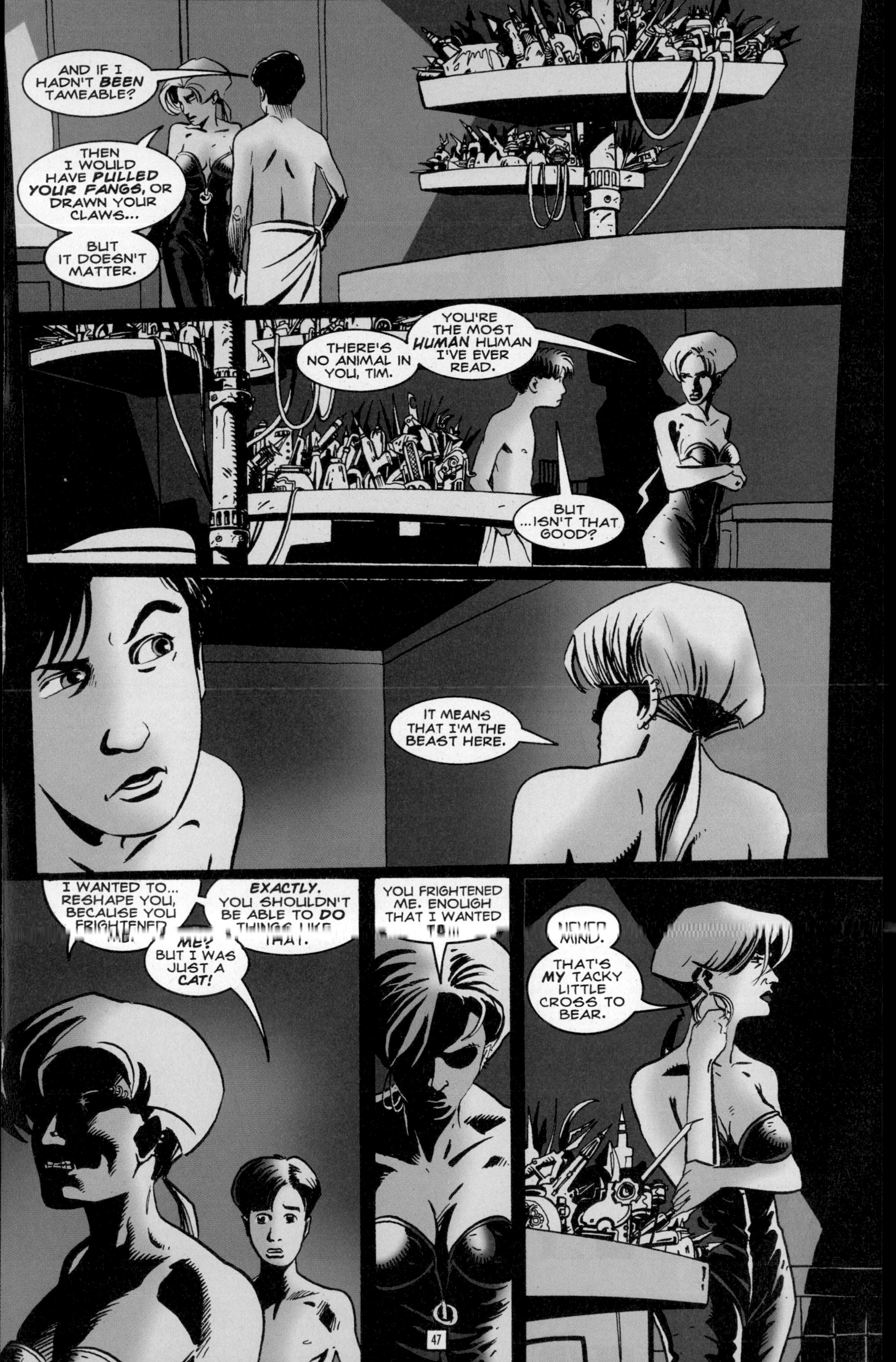
AND IF I HADN'T **BEEN** TAMEABLE?
THEN I WOULD HAVE **PULLED YOUR FANGS**, OR DRAWN YOUR CLAWS...
BUT IT DOESN'T MATTER.
THERE'S NO ANIMAL IN YOU, TIM.
YOU'RE THE MOST **HUMAN** HUMAN I'VE EVER READ.
BUT ...ISN'T THAT GOOD?
IT MEANS THAT I'M THE BEAST HERE.
I WANTED TO... RESHAPE YOU, BECAUSE YOU FRIGHTENED
EXACTLY. YOU SHOULDN'T BE ABLE TO **DO** THINGS LIKE THAT.
ME? BUT I WAS JUST A **CAT!**
YOU FRIGHTENED ME. ENOUGH THAT I WANTED
MIND.
THAT'S **MY** TACKY LITTLE CROSS TO BEAR.

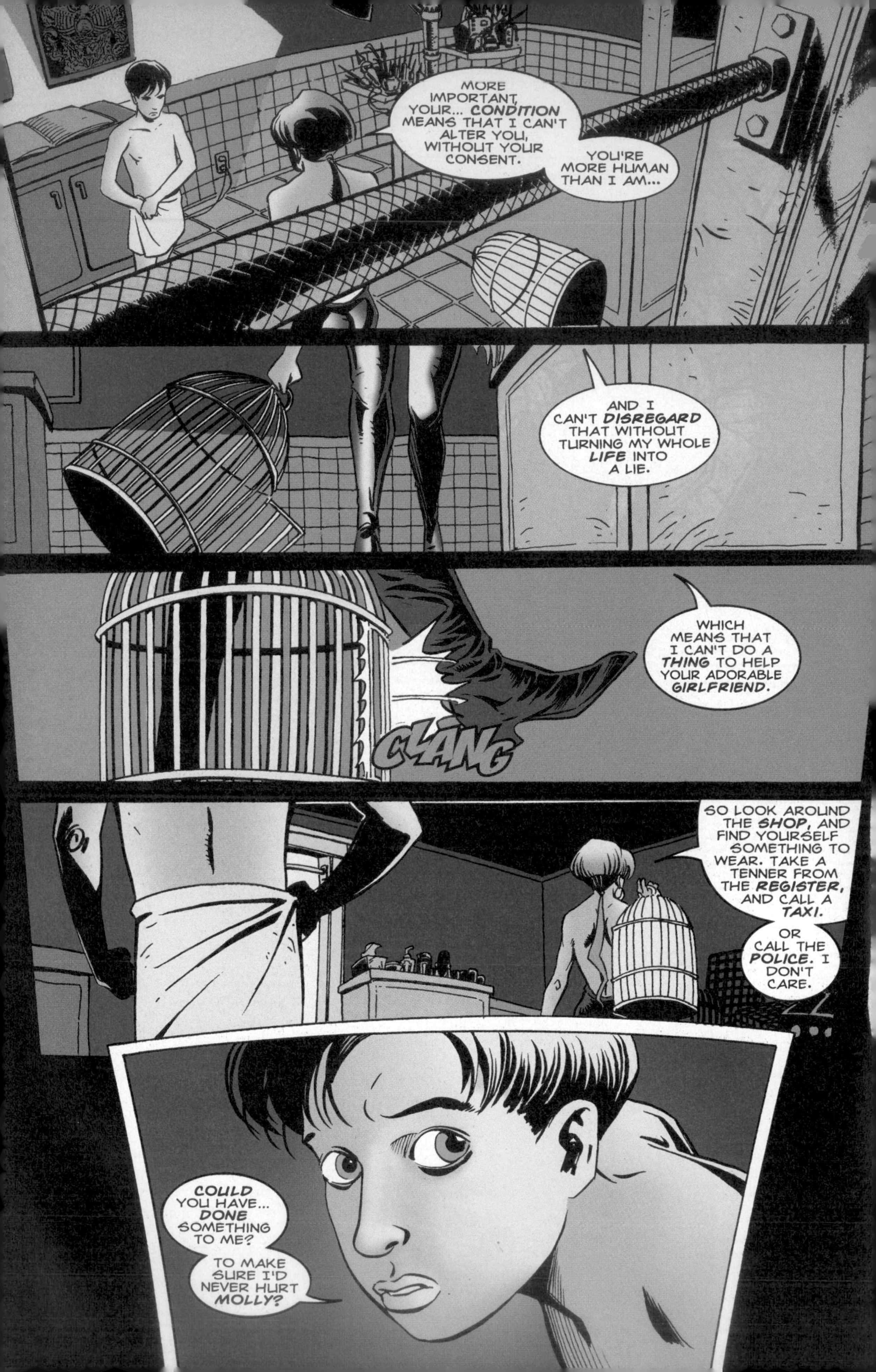
MORE IMPORTANT, YOUR... CONDITION MEANS THAT I CAN'T ALTER YOU, WITHOUT YOUR CONSENT.
YOU'RE MORE HUMAN THAN I AM...
AND I CAN'T DISREGARD THAT WITHOUT TURNING MY WHOLE LIFE INTO A LIE.
WHICH MEANS THAT I CAN'T DO A THING TO HELP YOUR ADORABLE GIRLFRIEND.
CLANG
SO LOOK AROUND THE SHOP, AND FIND YOURSELF SOMETHING TO WEAR. TAKE A TENNER FROM THE REGISTER, AND CALL A TAXI.
OR CALL THE POLICE. I DON'T CARE.
COULD YOU HAVE... DONE SOMETHING TO ME?
TO MAKE SURE I'D NEVER HURT MOLLY?

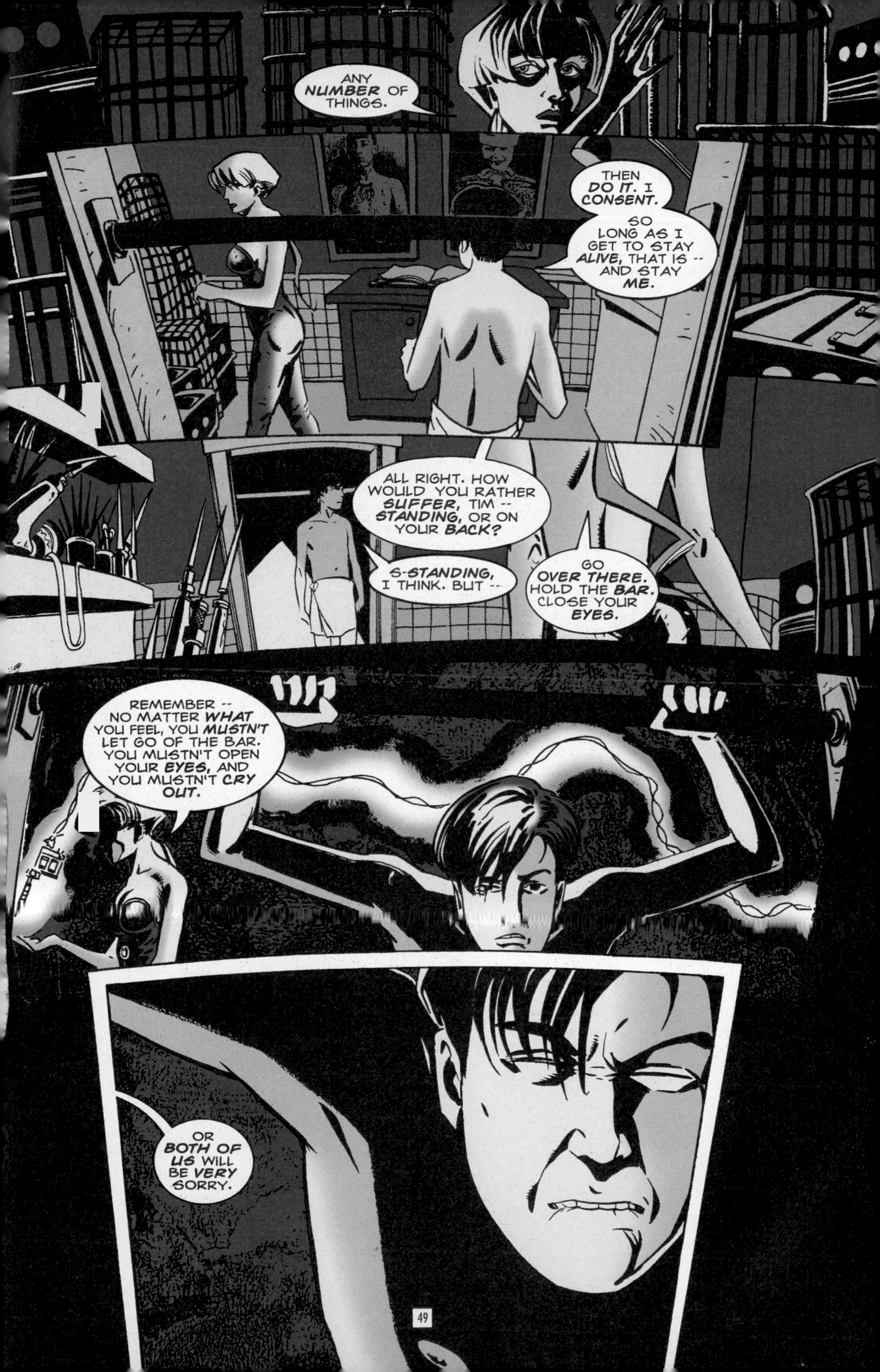
ANY NUMBER OF THINGS.
THEN DO IT. I CONSENT.
SO LONG AS I GET TO STAY ALIVE, THAT IS -- AND STAY ME.
ALL RIGHT. HOW WOULD YOU RATHER SUFFER, TIM -- STANDING, OR ON YOUR BACK?
S-STANDING, I THINK. BUT --
GO OVER THERE. HOLD THE BAR. CLOSE YOUR EYES.
REMEMBER -- NO MATTER WHAT YOU FEEL, YOU MUSTN'T LET GO OF THE BAR. YOU MUSTN'T OPEN YOUR EYES, AND YOU MUSTN'T CRY OUT.
OR BOTH OF US WILL BE VERY SORRY.

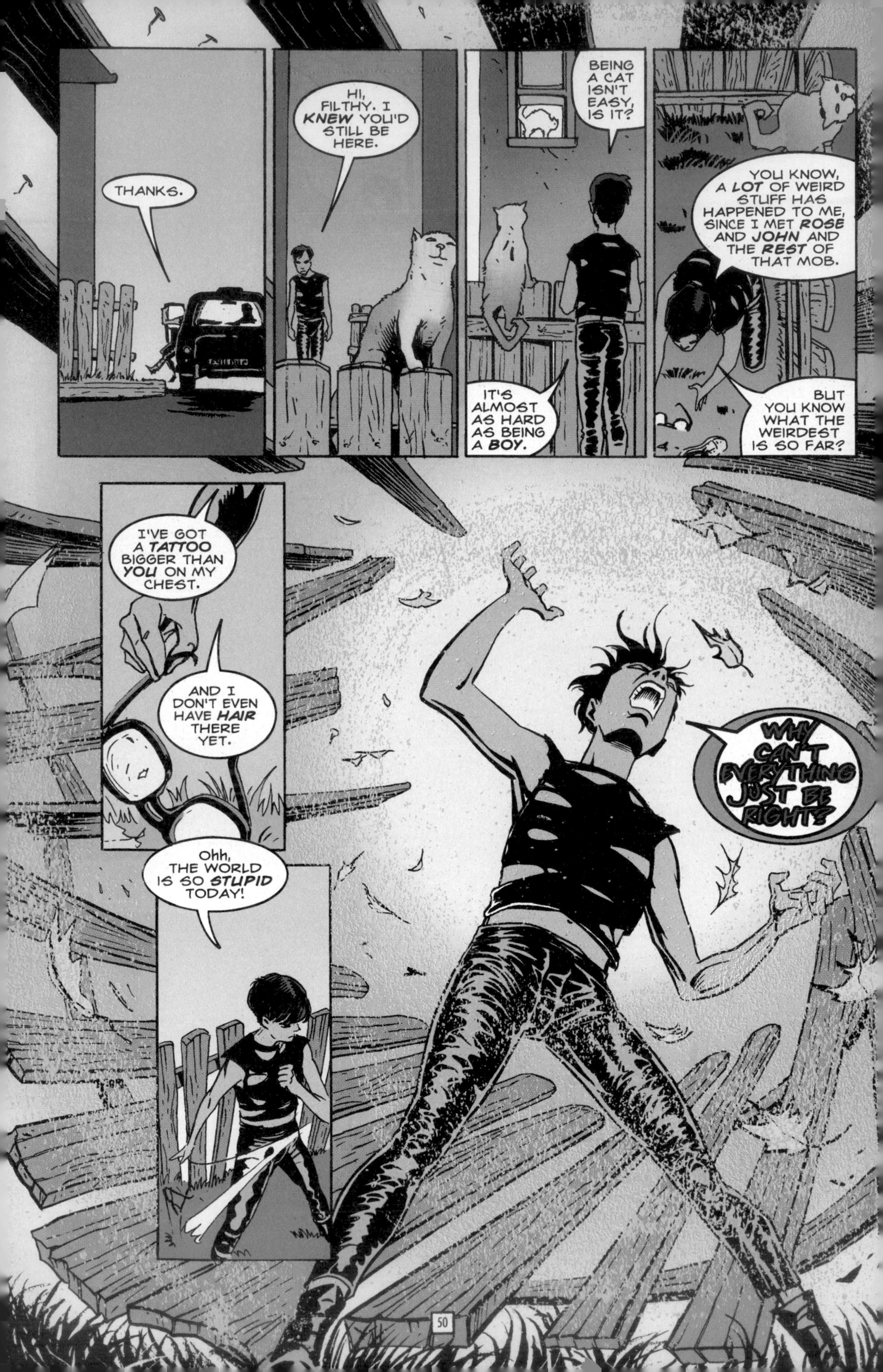
THANKS.
HI, FILTHY. I KNEW YOU'D STILL BE HERE.
BEING A CAT ISN'T EASY, IS IT?
IT'S ALMOST AS HARD AS BEING A BOY.
YOU KNOW, A LOT OF WEIRD STUFF HAS HAPPENED TO ME, SINCE I MET ROSE AND JOHN AND THE REST OF THAT MOB.
BUT YOU KNOW WHAT THE WEIRDEST IS SO FAR?
I'VE GOT A TATTOO BIGGER THAN YOU ON MY CHEST.
AND I DON'T EVEN HAVE HAIR THERE YET.
Ohh, THE WORLD IS SO STUPID TODAY!
WHY CAN'T EVERYTHING JUST BE RIGHT?

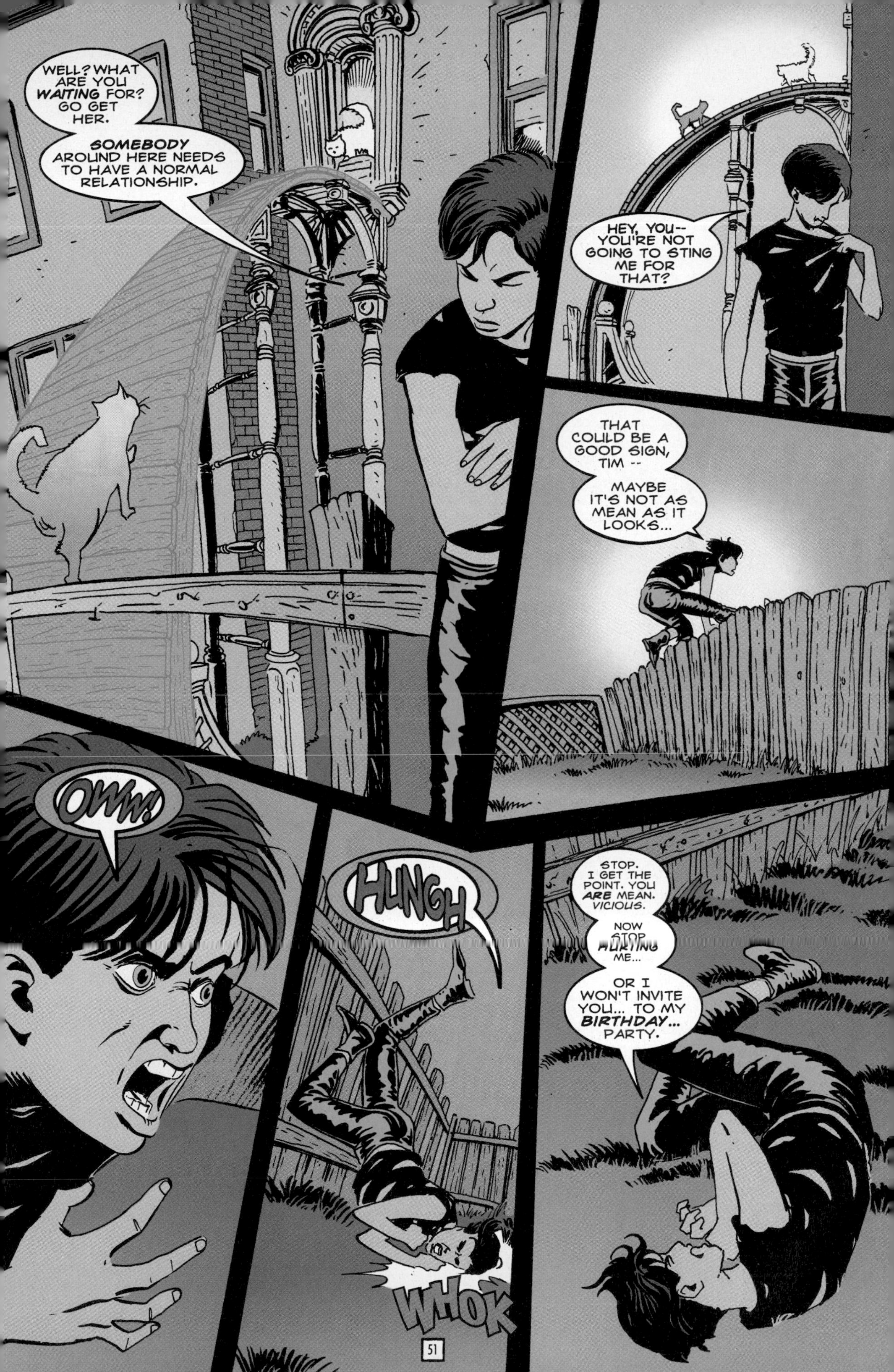
WELL? WHAT ARE YOU WAITING FOR? GO GET HER.
SOMEBODY AROUND HERE NEEDS TO HAVE A NORMAL RELATIONSHIP.
HEY, YOU-- YOU'RE NOT GOING TO STING ME FOR THAT?
THAT COULD BE A GOOD SIGN, TIM --
MAYBE IT'S NOT AS MEAN AS IT LOOKS...
OWW!
HUNGH
WHOK
STOP. I GET THE POINT. YOU ARE MEAN. VICIOUS.
NOW STOP HURTING ME...
OR I WON'T INVITE YOU... TO MY BIRTHDAY... PARTY.

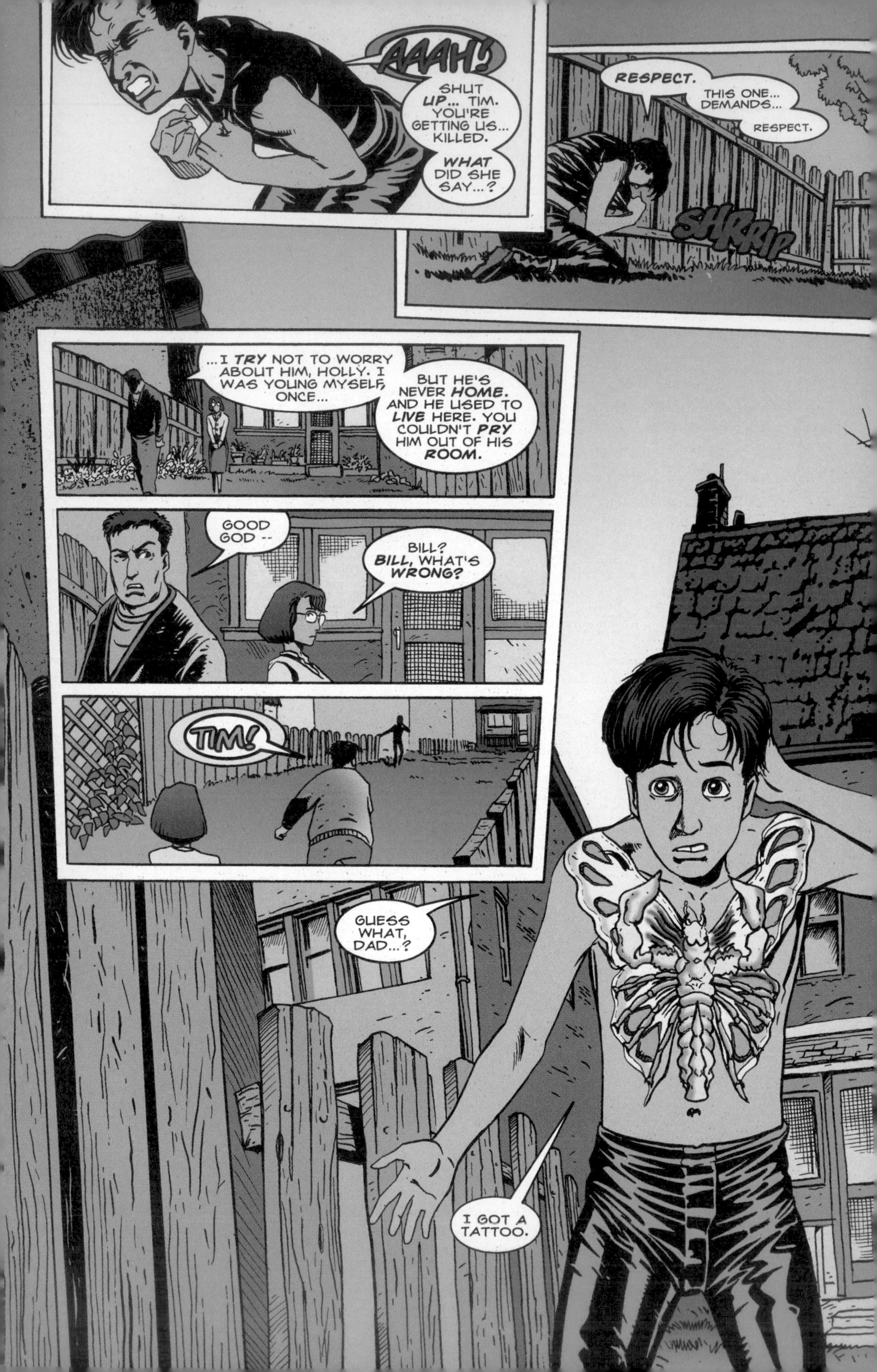
AAAH!
SHUT UP... TIM. YOU'RE GETTING US... KILLED.
WHAT DID SHE SAY...?
RESPECT.
THIS ONE... DEMANDS...
RESPECT.
SHRRIP
...I TRY NOT TO WORRY ABOUT HIM, HOLLY. I WAS YOUNG MYSELF, ONCE...
BUT HE'S NEVER HOME. AND HE USED TO LIVE HERE. YOU COULDN'T PRY HIM OUT OF HIS ROOM.
GOOD GOD --
BILL? BILL, WHAT'S WRONG?
TIM!
GUESS WHAT, DAD...?
I GOT A TATTOO.

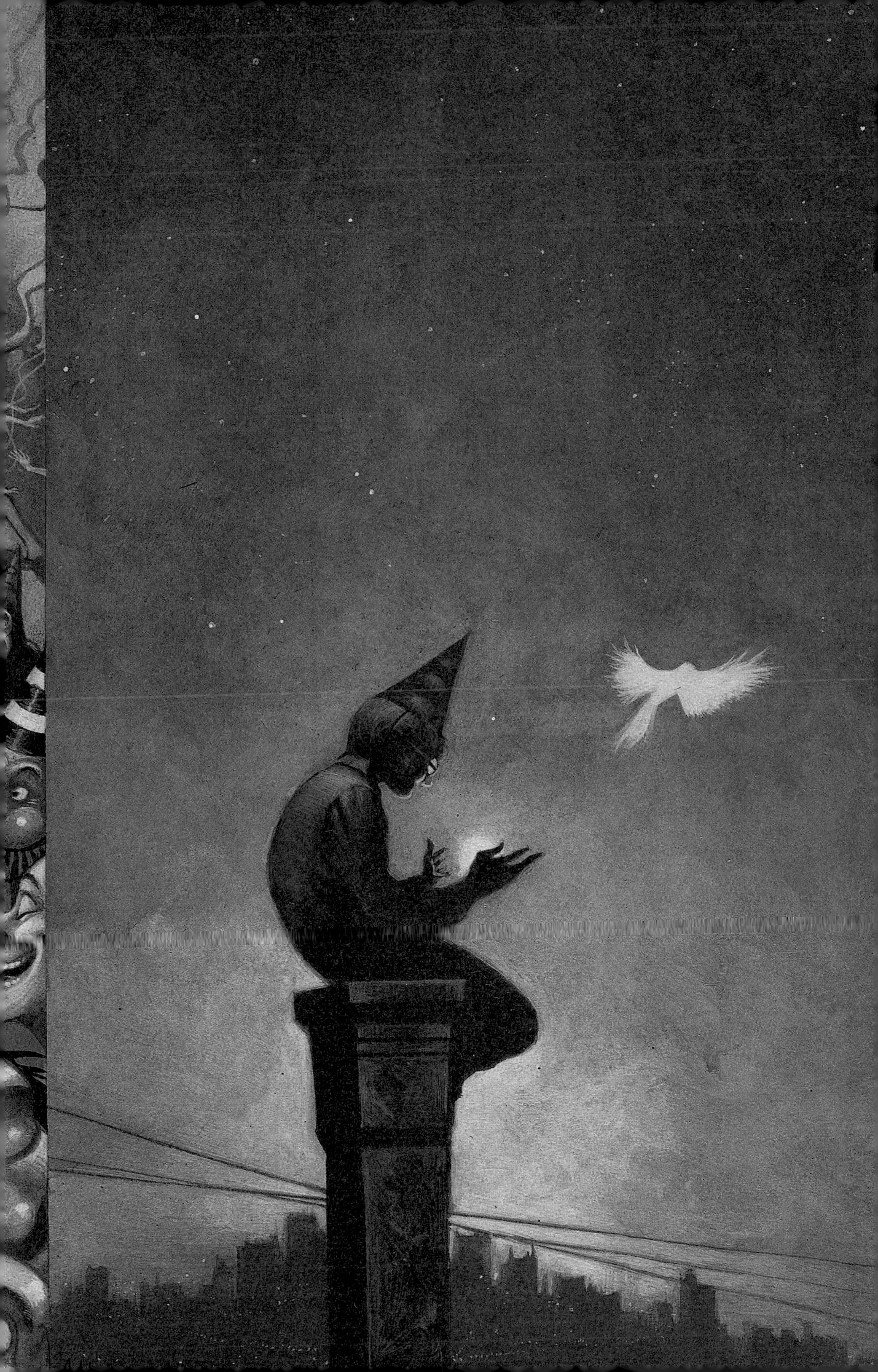

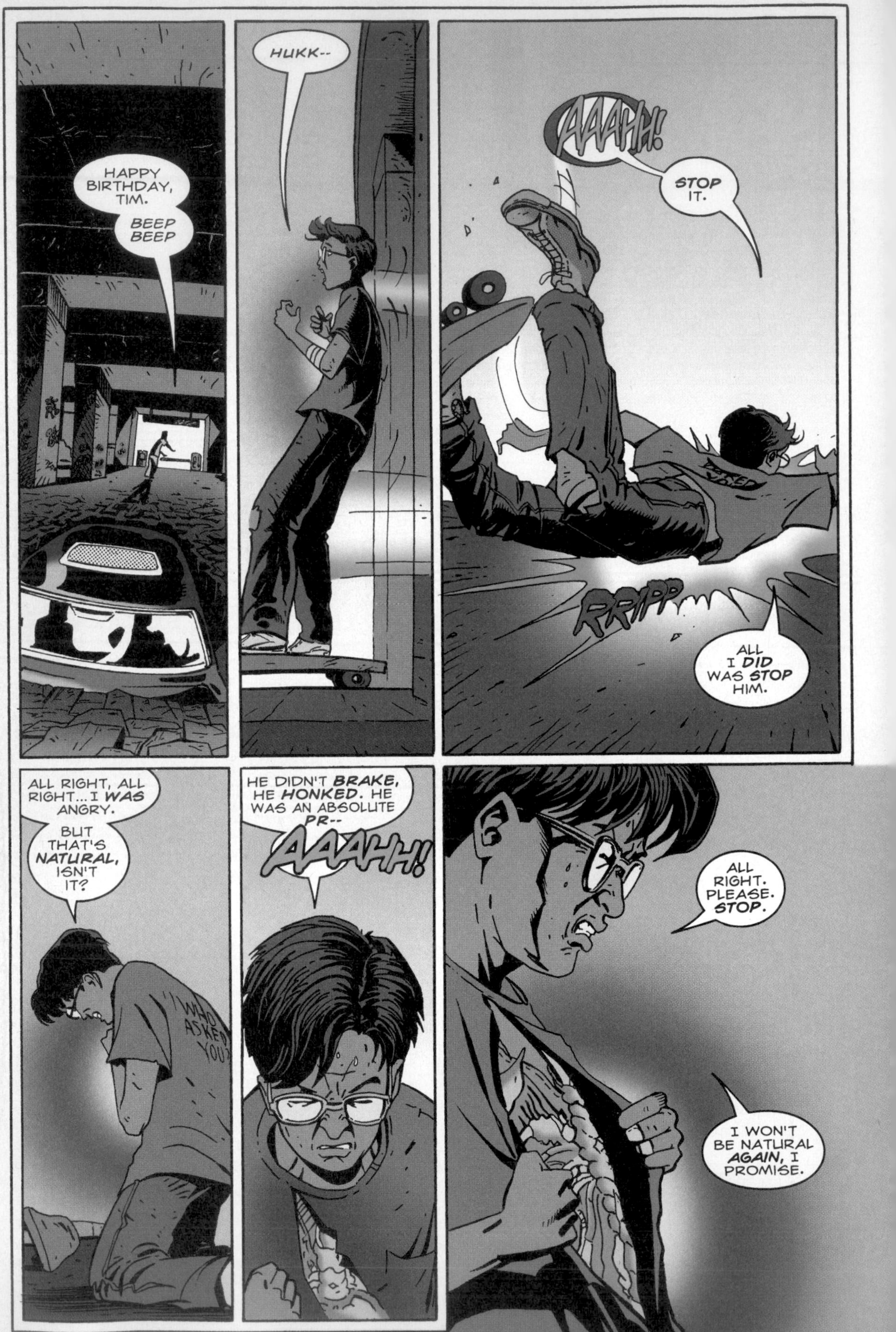
HAPPY BIRTHDAY, TIM.
BEEP BEEP
HUKK--
AAAHH!
STOP IT.
RRIPP
ALL I DID WAS STOP HIM.
ALL RIGHT, ALL RIGHT... I WAS ANGRY.
BUT THAT'S NATURAL, ISN'T IT?
WHO ASKED YOU?
HE DIDN'T BRAKE, HE HONKED. HE WAS AN ABSOLUTE PR--
AAAHH!
ALL RIGHT. PLEASE. STOP.
I WON'T BE NATURAL AGAIN, I PROMISE.

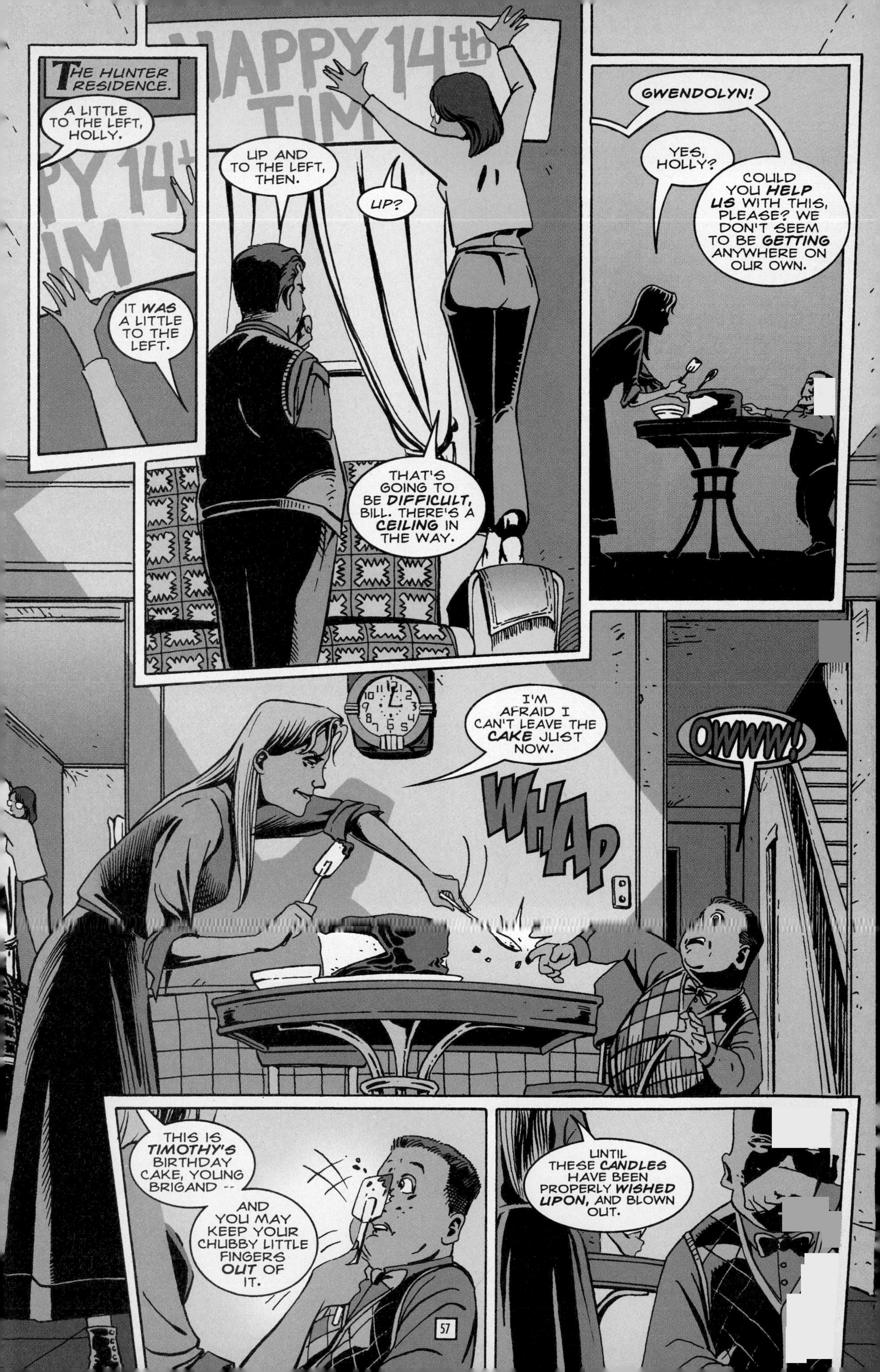
THE HUNTER RESIDENCE.
A LITTLE TO THE LEFT, HOLLY.
IT WAS A LITTLE TO THE LEFT.
HAPPY 14th TIM
UP AND TO THE LEFT, THEN.
UP?
THAT'S GOING TO BE DIFFICULT, BILL. THERE'S A CEILING IN THE WAY.
GWENDOLYN!
YES, HOLLY?
COULD YOU HELP US WITH THIS, PLEASE? WE DON'T SEEM TO BE GETTING ANYWHERE ON OUR OWN.
I'M AFRAID I CAN'T LEAVE THE CAKE JUST NOW.
WHAP
OWWW!
THIS IS TIMOTHY'S BIRTHDAY CAKE, YOUNG BRIGAND --
AND YOU MAY KEEP YOUR CHUBBY LITTLE FINGERS OUT OF IT.
UNTIL THESE CANDLES HAVE BEEN PROPERLY WISHED UPON, AND BLOWN OUT.

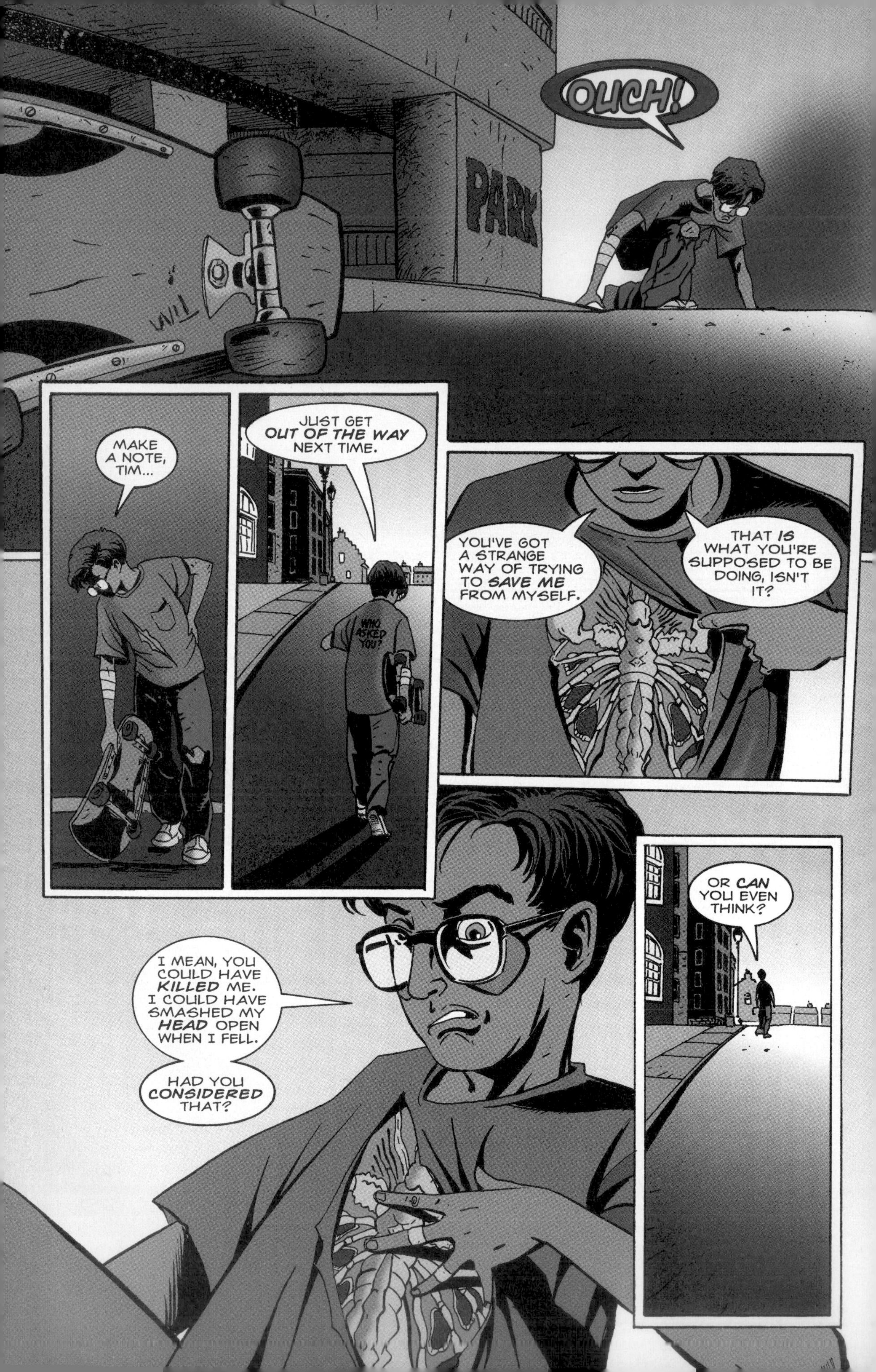
OUCH!
PARK
MAKE A NOTE, TIM...
JUST GET OUT OF THE WAY NEXT TIME.
WHO ASKED YOU?
YOU'VE GOT A STRANGE WAY OF TRYING TO SAVE ME FROM MYSELF.
THAT IS WHAT YOU'RE SUPPOSED TO BE DOING, ISN'T IT?
I MEAN, YOU COULD HAVE KILLED ME. I COULD HAVE SMASHED MY HEAD OPEN WHEN I FELL.
HAD YOU CONSIDERED THAT?
OR CAN YOU EVEN THINK?

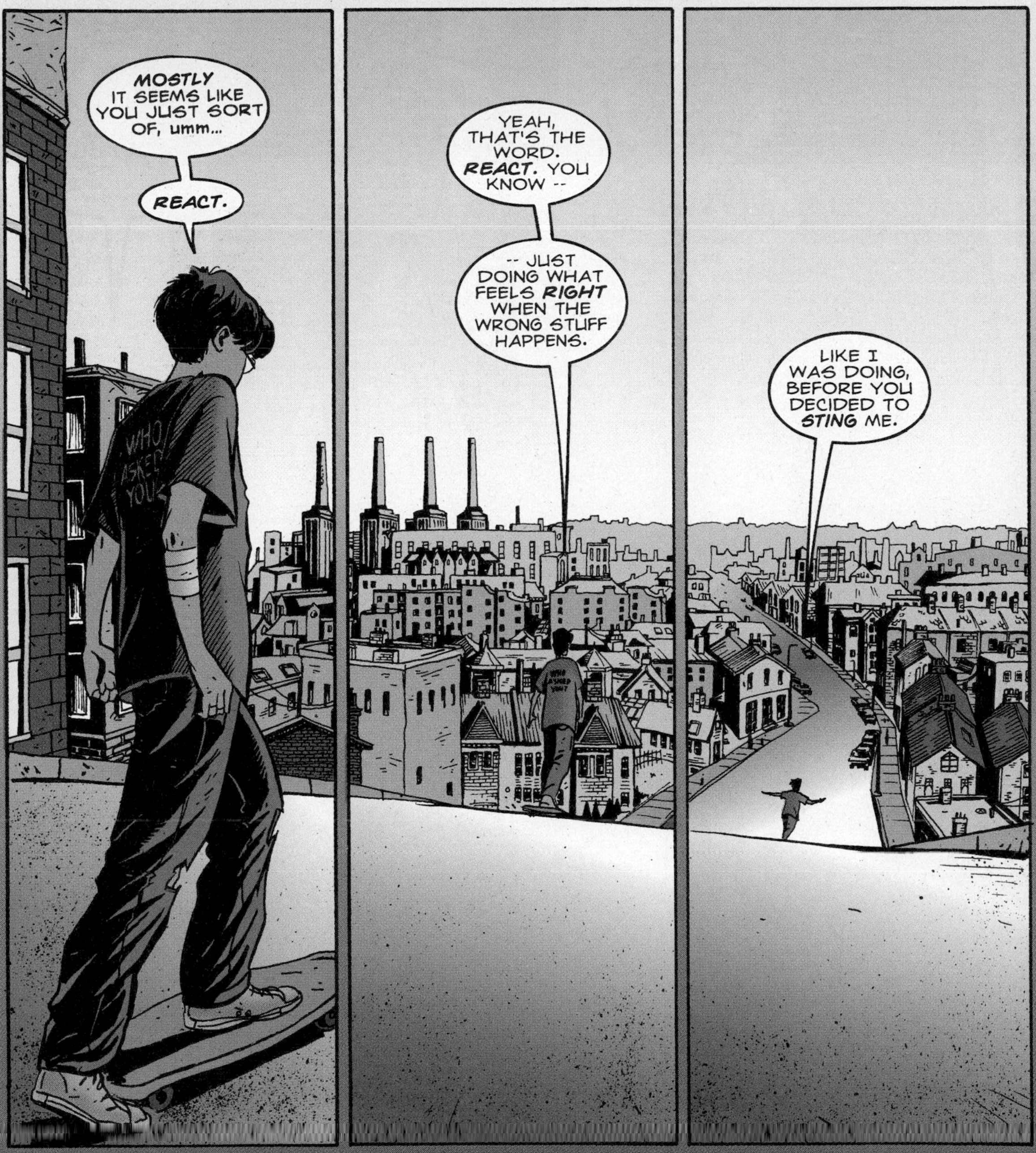
MOSTLY IT SEEMS LIKE YOU JUST SORT OF, umm...
REACT.
WHO ASKED YOU
YEAH, THAT'S THE WORD. REACT. YOU KNOW --
-- JUST DOING WHAT FEELS RIGHT WHEN THE WRONG STUFF HAPPENS.
LIKE I WAS DOING, BEFORE YOU DECIDED TO STING ME.

Red Rover, Red Rover.

John Ney Rieber *writer* · Peter Gross *artist* · Neil Gaiman *consultant*

Sherilyn van Valkenburgh *colorist* · Richard Starkings AND Comicraft *lettering* · Julie Rottenberg *editor*

Timothy Hunter and the *Books of Magic* created by *Neil Gaiman & John Bolton*

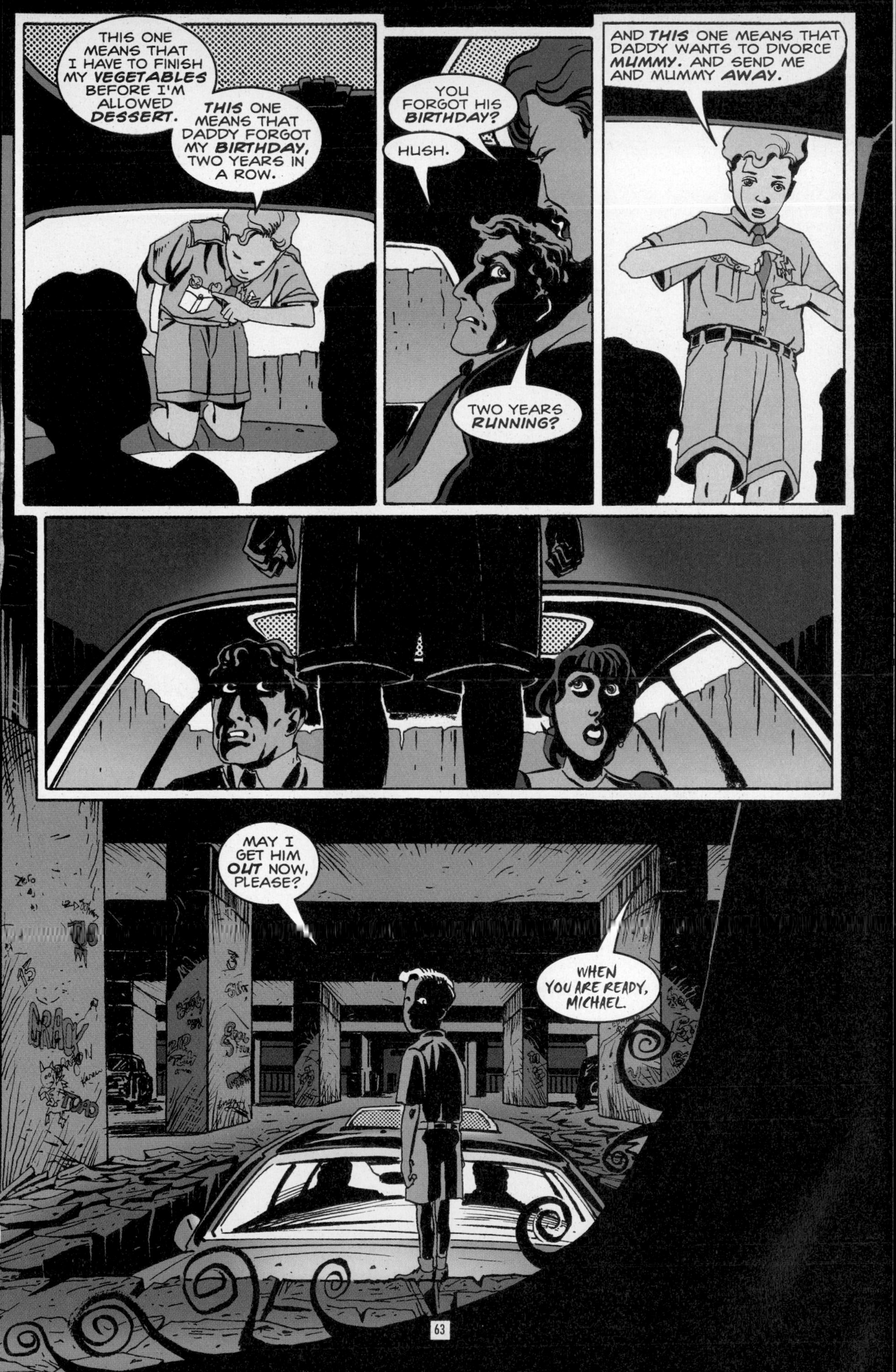
THIS ONE MEANS THAT I HAVE TO FINISH MY VEGETABLES BEFORE I'M ALLOWED DESSERT.
THIS ONE MEANS THAT DADDY FORGOT MY BIRTHDAY, TWO YEARS IN A ROW.
YOU FORGOT HIS BIRTHDAY?
HUSH.
TWO YEARS RUNNING?
AND THIS ONE MEANS THAT DADDY WANTS TO DIVORCE MUMMY. AND SEND ME AND MUMMY AWAY.
MAY I GET HIM OUT NOW, PLEASE?
WHEN YOU ARE READY, MICHAEL.

Cricket's Thimble
Fine Fabrics & Notions

Happy Birthday to me... Happy Birthday to me...

Happy Birthday running stupid errands... Happy Birthday to me...

Not.

Mrs. CRICKET?

THIS IS FOR YOU.

WELL?

YOU DON'T EXPECT ME TO CHASE YOU 'ROUND THE SHOP FOR IT, I HOPE.

Aah, THIS IS FROM MISS GWENDOLYN, ISN'T IT? YOU DON'T SEE HANDWRITING AS FINE AS HERS, THESE DAYS.

OR STITCHWORK, FOR THAT MATTER. OOO, SHE COULD TAT LACE IN HER SLEEP, THAT GIRL.

MIND THE COUNTER, HANDS OFF THE TILL...

FABRIC SALE
BOLT ENDS 33% OFF

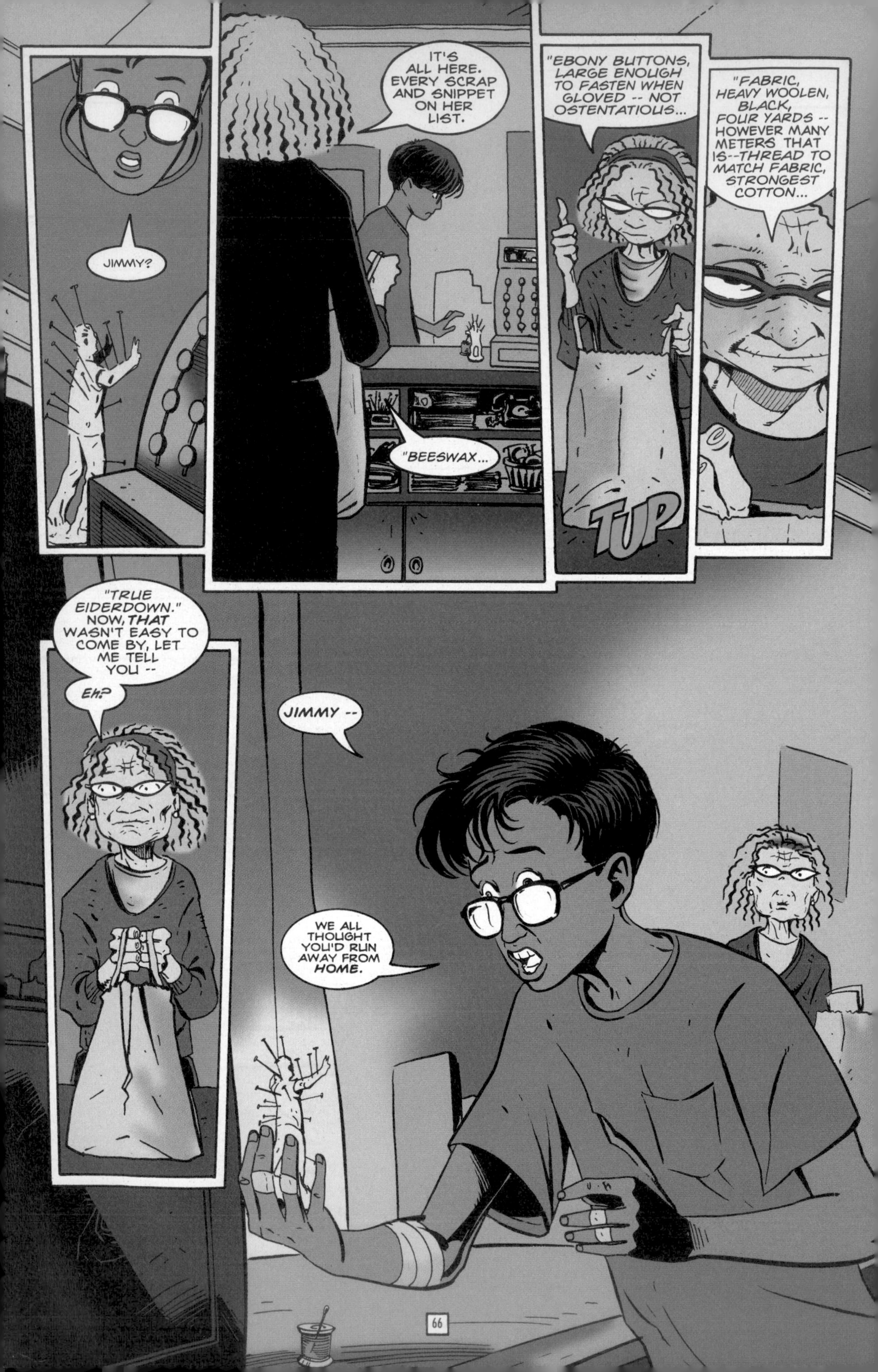
JIMMY?
IT'S ALL HERE. EVERY SCRAP AND SNIPPET ON HER LIST.
"BEESWAX...
"EBONY BUTTONS, LARGE ENOUGH TO FASTEN WHEN GLOVED -- NOT OSTENTATIOUS...
TUP
"FABRIC, HEAVY WOOLEN, BLACK, FOUR YARDS -- HOWEVER MANY METERS THAT IS--THREAD TO MATCH FABRIC, STRONGEST COTTON...
"TRUE EIDERDOWN." NOW, THAT WASN'T EASY TO COME BY, LET ME TELL YOU --
Eh?
JIMMY --
WE ALL THOUGHT YOU'D RUN AWAY FROM HOME.

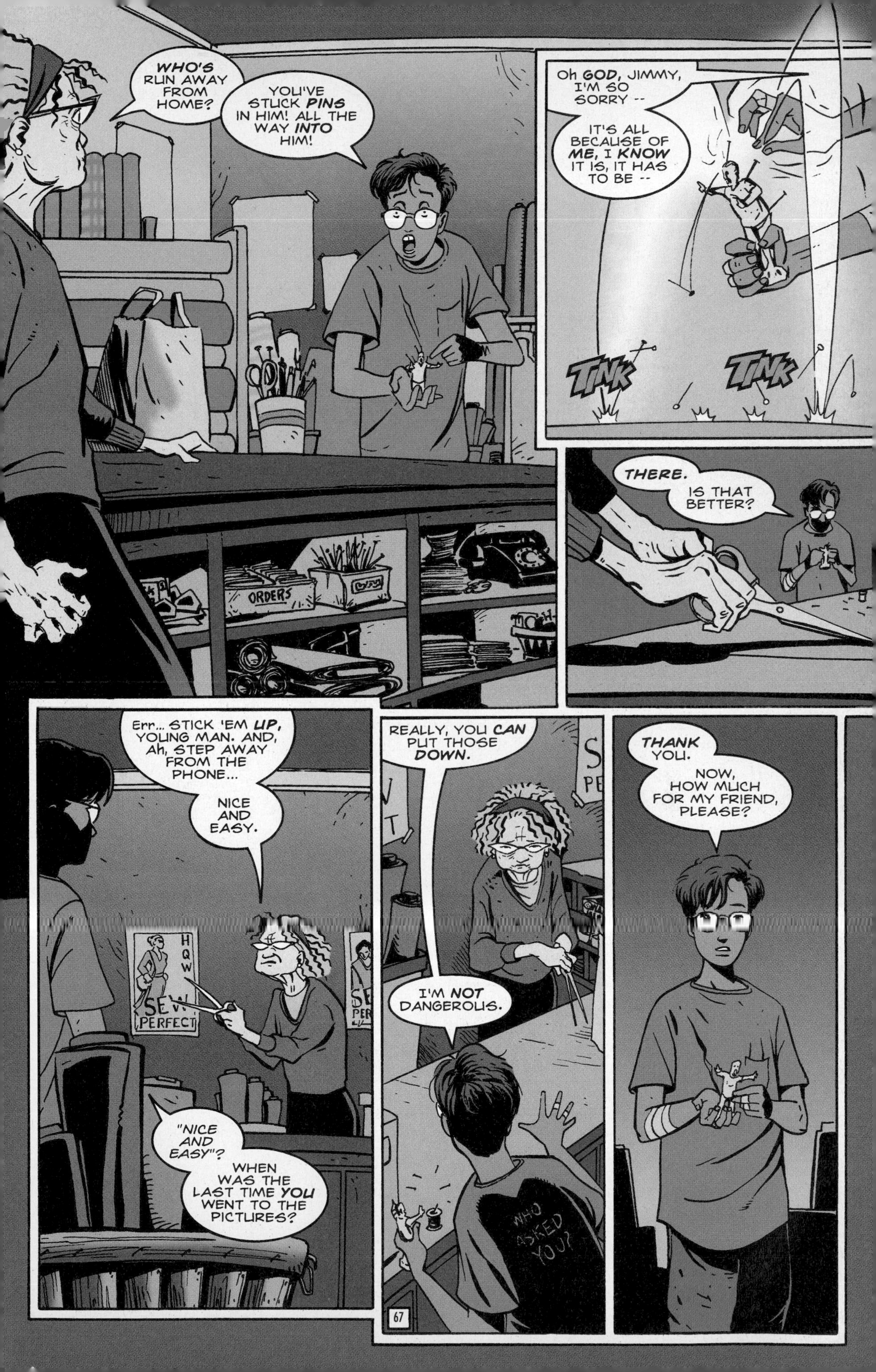
WHO'S RUN AWAY FROM HOME?
YOU'VE STUCK PINS IN HIM! ALL THE WAY INTO HIM!
Oh GOD, JIMMY, I'M SO SORRY --
IT'S ALL BECAUSE OF ME, I KNOW IT IS, IT HAS TO BE --
TINK
TINK
THERE. IS THAT BETTER?
ORDERS
Err... STICK 'EM UP, YOUNG MAN. AND, Ah, STEP AWAY FROM THE PHONE...
NICE AND EASY.
SEW PERFECT
"NICE AND EASY"? WHEN WAS THE LAST TIME YOU WENT TO THE PICTURES?
REALLY, YOU CAN PUT THOSE DOWN.
I'M NOT DANGEROUS.
WHO ASKED YOU?
THANK YOU.
NOW, HOW MUCH FOR MY FRIEND, PLEASE?

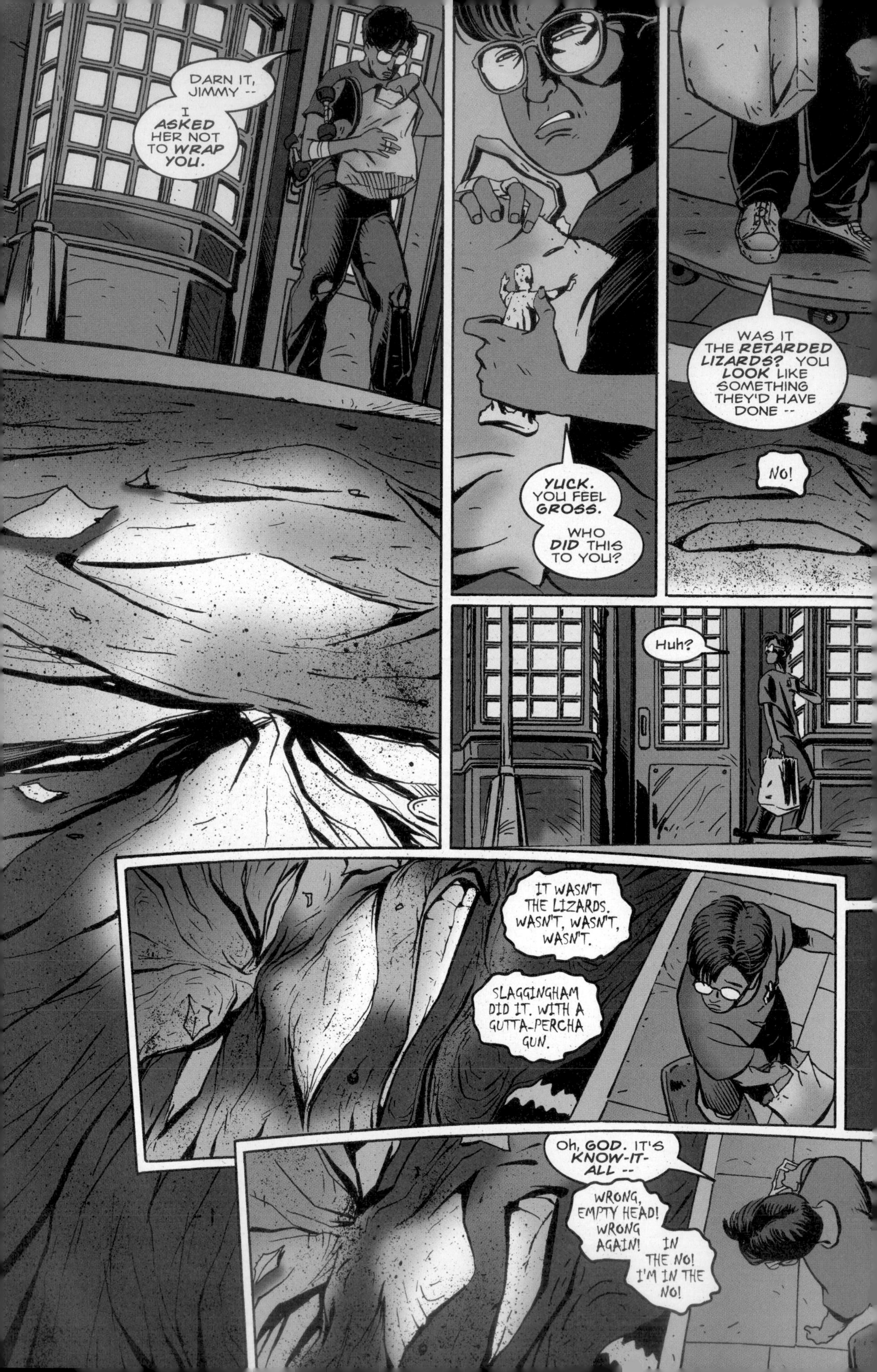
DARN IT, JIMMY -- I ASKED HER NOT TO WRAP YOU.
YUCK. YOU FEEL GROSS.
WHO DID THIS TO YOU?
WAS IT THE RETARDED LIZARDS? YOU LOOK LIKE SOMETHING THEY'D HAVE DONE --
NO!
Huh?
IT WASN'T THE LIZARDS. WASN'T, WASN'T, WASN'T.
SLAGGINGHAM DID IT. WITH A GUTTA-PERCHA GUN.
Oh, GOD. IT'S KNOW-IT-ALL --
WRONG, EMPTY HEAD! WRONG AGAIN!
IN THE NO! I'M IN THE NO!

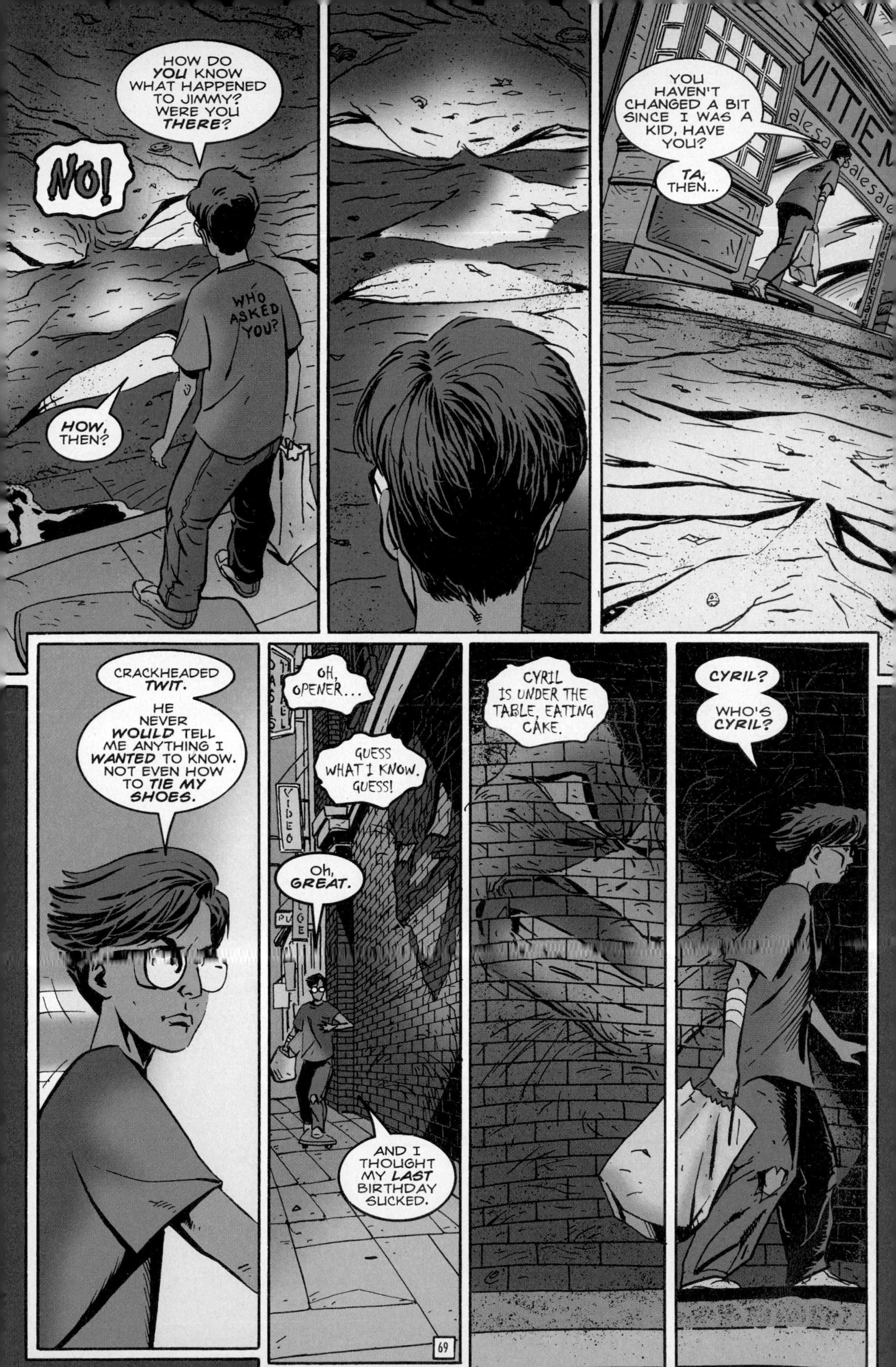
HOW DO YOU KNOW WHAT HAPPENED TO JIMMY? WERE YOU THERE?
NO!
WHO ASKED YOU?
HOW, THEN?
YOU HAVEN'T CHANGED A BIT SINCE I WAS A KID, HAVE YOU?
TA, THEN...
CRACKHEADED TWIT.
HE NEVER WOULD TELL ME ANYTHING I WANTED TO KNOW. NOT EVEN HOW TO TIE MY SHOES.
OH, OPENER...
GUESS WHAT I KNOW. GUESS!
VIDEO
Oh, GREAT.
AND I THOUGHT MY LAST BIRTHDAY SUCKED.
CYRIL IS UNDER THE TABLE, EATING CAKE.
CYRIL?
WHO'S CYRIL?

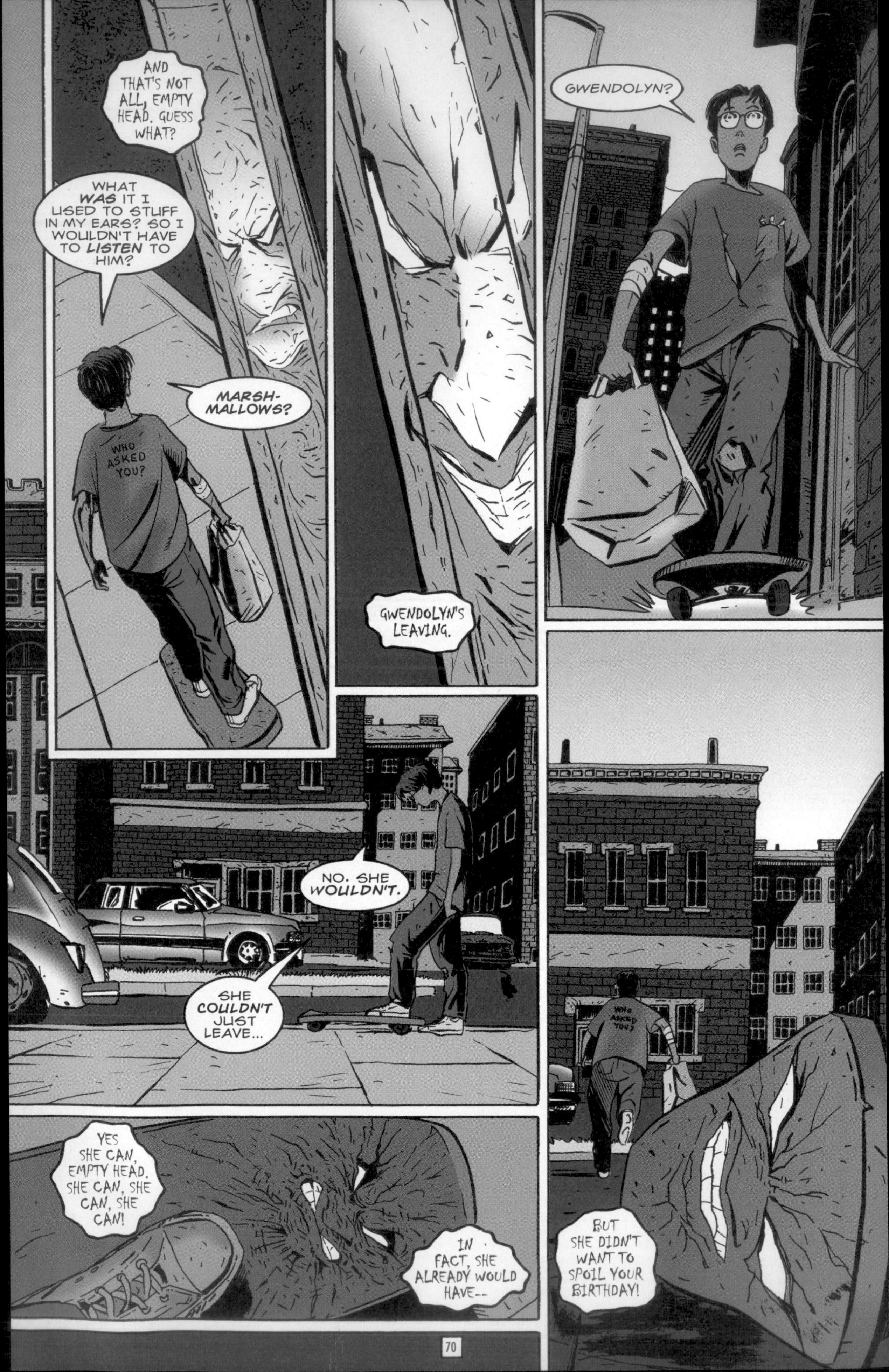
AND THAT'S NOT ALL, EMPTY HEAD. GUESS WHAT?
WHAT WAS IT I USED TO STUFF IN MY EARS? SO I WOULDN'T HAVE TO LISTEN TO HIM?
MARSH-MALLOWS?
WHO ASKED YOU?
GWENDOLYN'S LEAVING.
GWENDOLYN?
NO. SHE WOULDN'T.
SHE COULDN'T JUST LEAVE...
YES SHE CAN, EMPTY HEAD. SHE CAN, SHE CAN, SHE CAN!
IN FACT, SHE ALREADY WOULD HAVE--
BUT SHE DIDN'T WANT TO SPOIL YOUR BIRTHDAY!

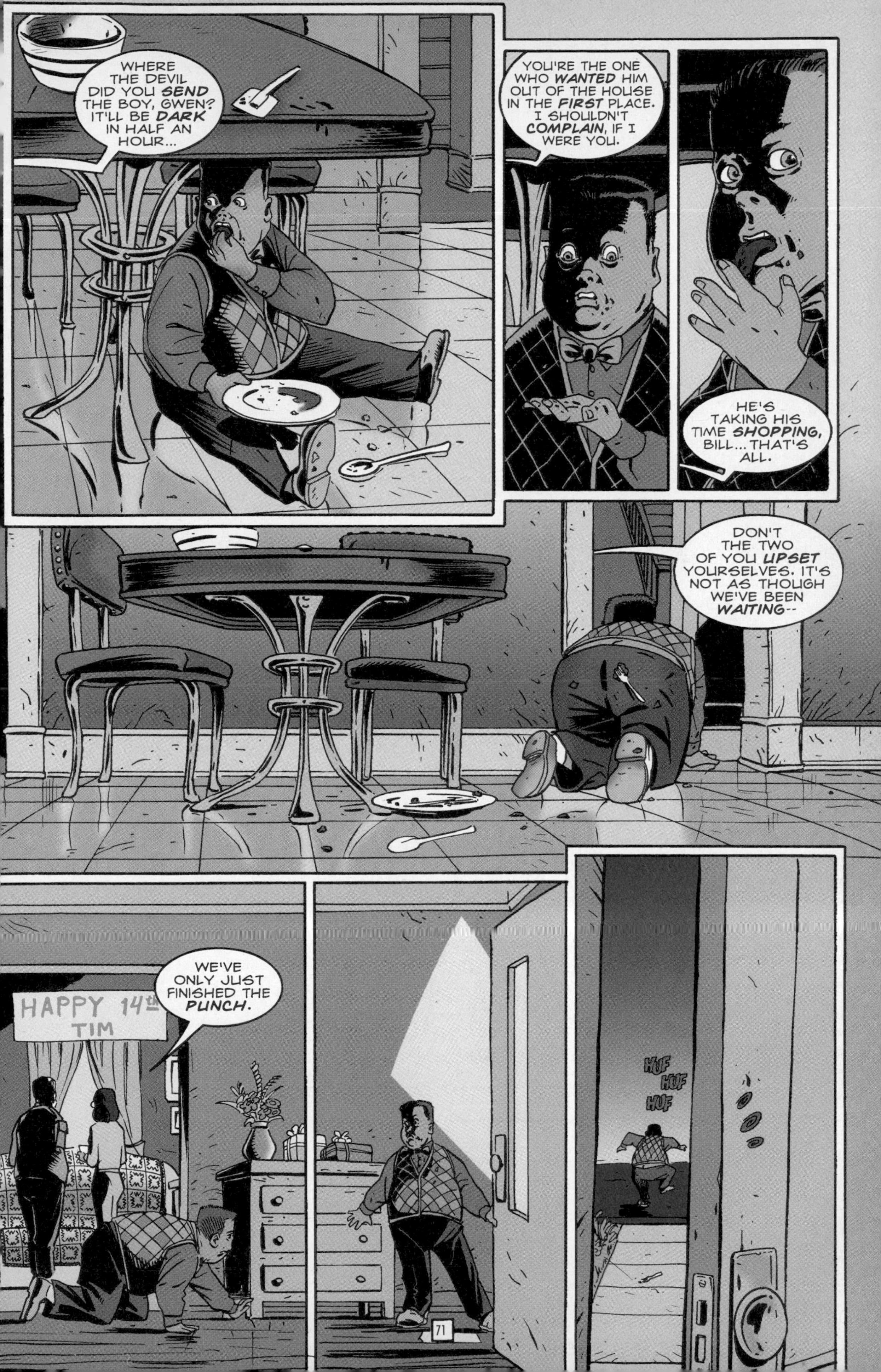

WHERE THE DEVIL DID YOU SEND THE BOY, GWEN? IT'LL BE DARK IN HALF AN HOUR...
YOU'RE THE ONE WHO WANTED HIM OUT OF THE HOUSE IN THE FIRST PLACE. I SHOULDN'T COMPLAIN, IF I WERE YOU.
HE'S TAKING HIS TIME SHOPPING, BILL... THAT'S ALL.
DON'T THE TWO OF YOU UPSET YOURSELVES. IT'S NOT AS THOUGH WE'VE BEEN WAITING--
HAPPY 14th TIM
WE'VE ONLY JUST FINISHED THE PUNCH.
HUF
HUF
HUF

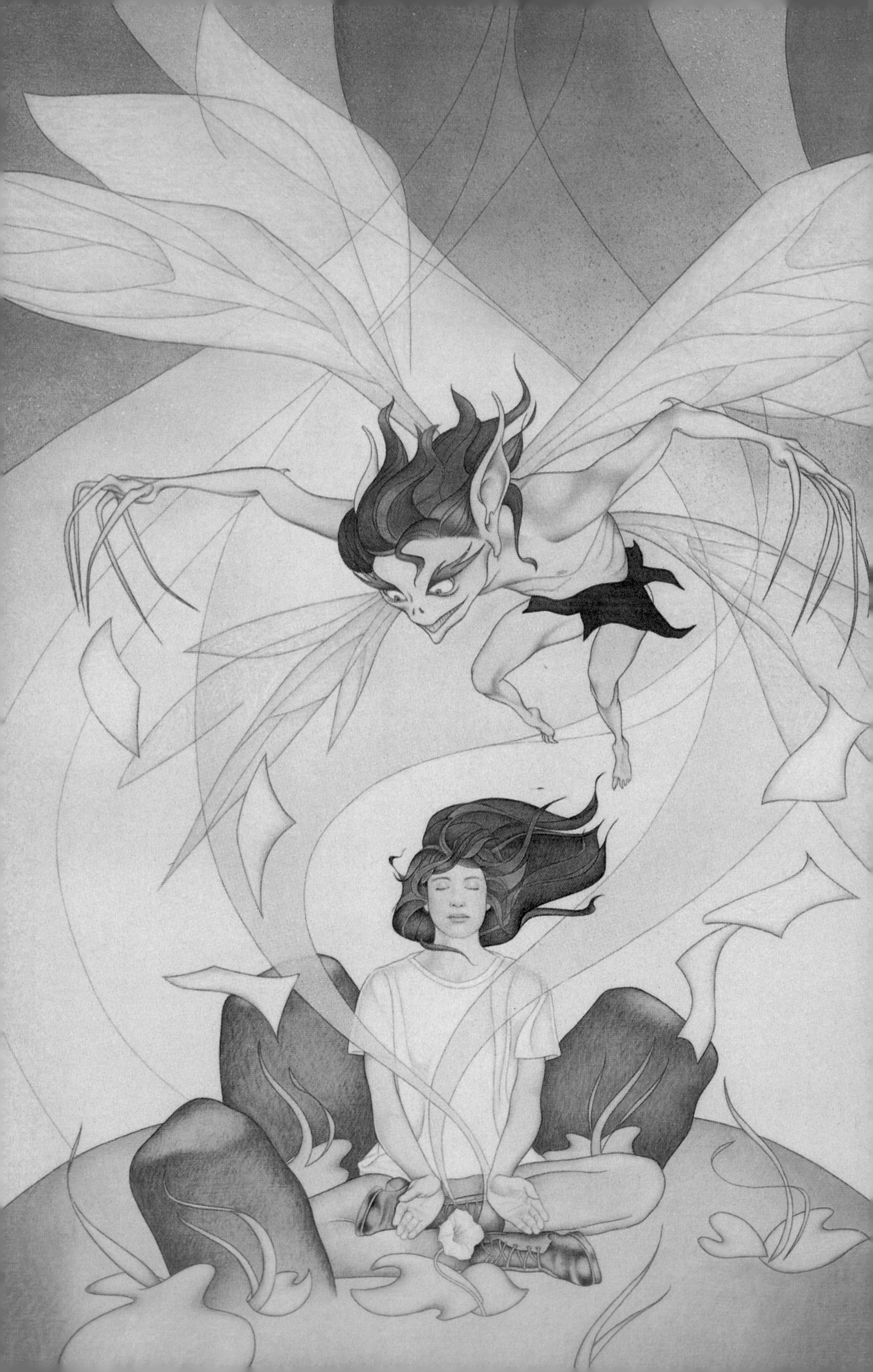

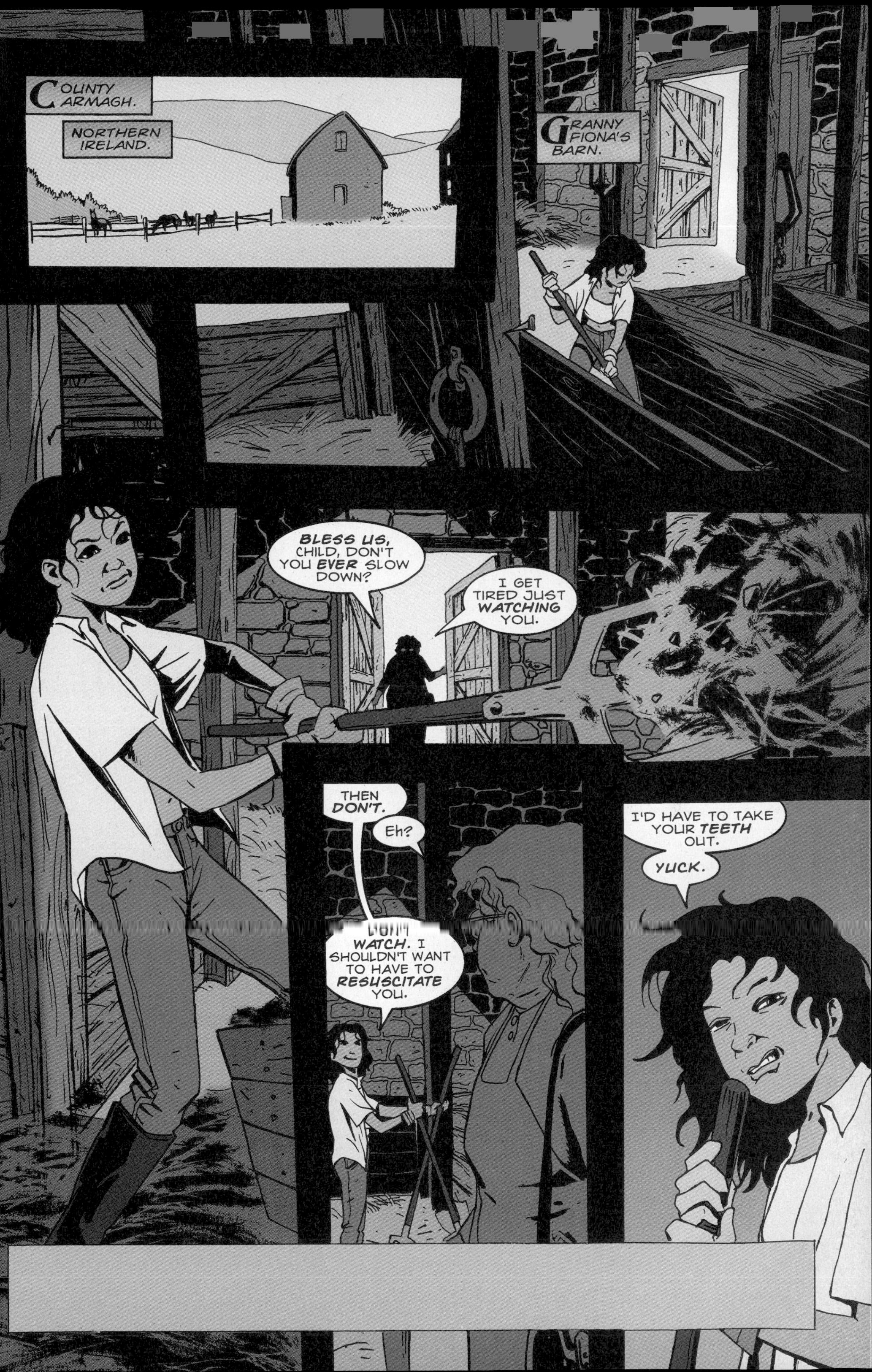
COUNTY ARMAGH.
NORTHERN IRELAND.
GRANNY FIONA'S BARN.
BLESS US, CHILD, DON'T YOU EVER SLOW DOWN?
I GET TIRED JUST WATCHING YOU.
THEN DON'T.
Eh?
WATCH. I SHOULDN'T WANT TO HAVE TO RESUSCITATE YOU.
I'D HAVE TO TAKE YOUR TEETH OUT.
YUCK.

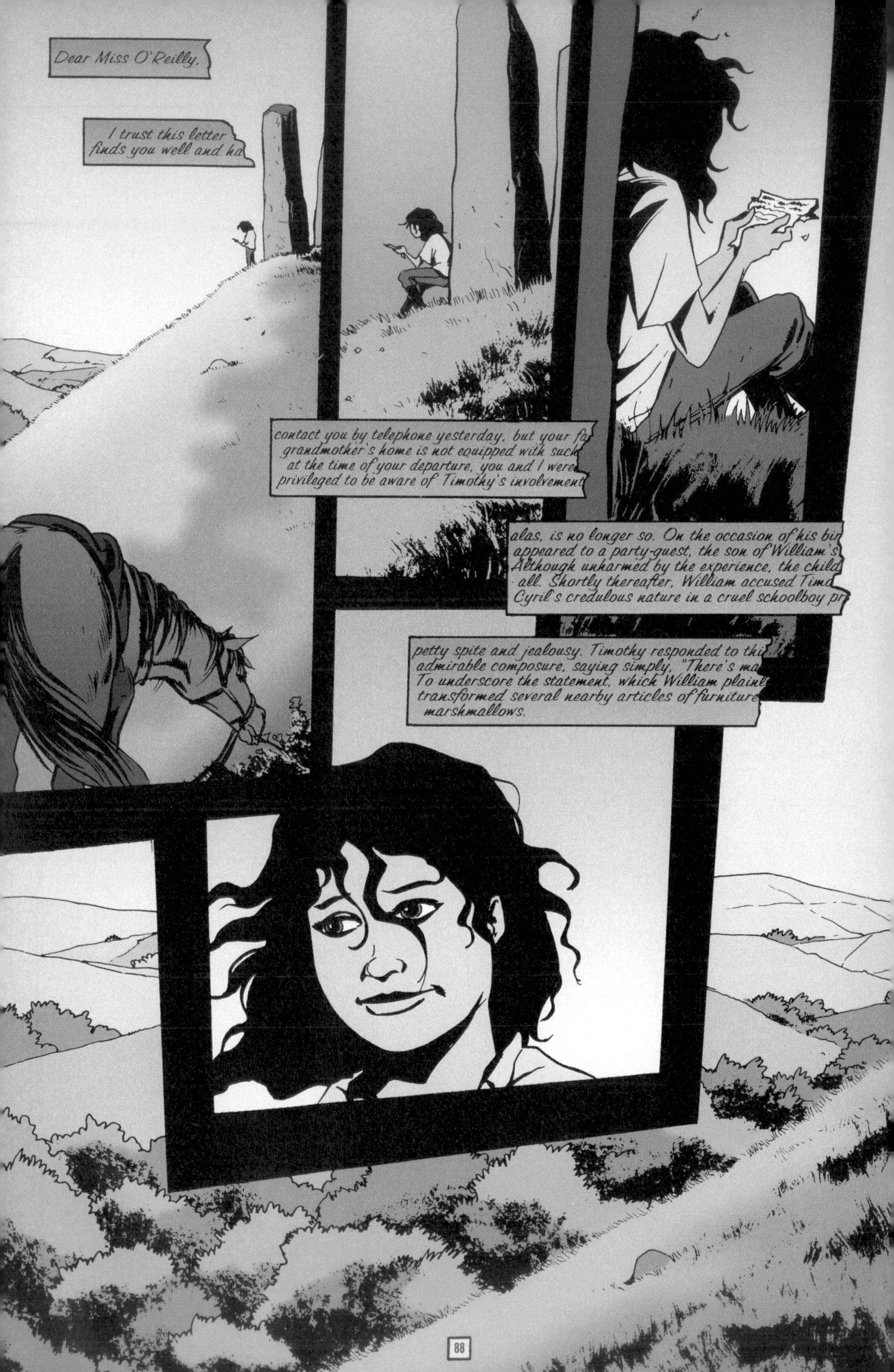
Dear Miss O'Reilly,
I trust this letter finds you well and ha
contact you by telephone yesterday, but your fa grandmother's home is not equipped with such at the time of your departure, you and I were privileged to be aware of Timothy's involvement
alas, is no longer so. On the occasion of his bi appeared to a party-guest, the son of William's Although unharmed by the experience, the child all. Shortly thereafter, William accused Timo Cyril's credulous nature in a cruel schoolboy pr
petty spite and jealousy. Timothy responded to thi admirable composure, saying simply, "There's ma To underscore the statement, which William plainl transformed several nearby articles of furniture marshmallows.

HE MUST HAVE HEARD EVERYTHING I SAID.

HE WAS THERE.

IN THE PARK...

WELL.

I OWE HIM AN ICE CREAM. AND AN EXPLANATION.

AND HE'S GOING TO GET THEM. LIKE IT OR NOT.

TIM'S DAD MAY BE PERFECTLY WILLING TO LET HIM DISAPPEAR, BUT I'M NOT PUTTING UP WITH IT.

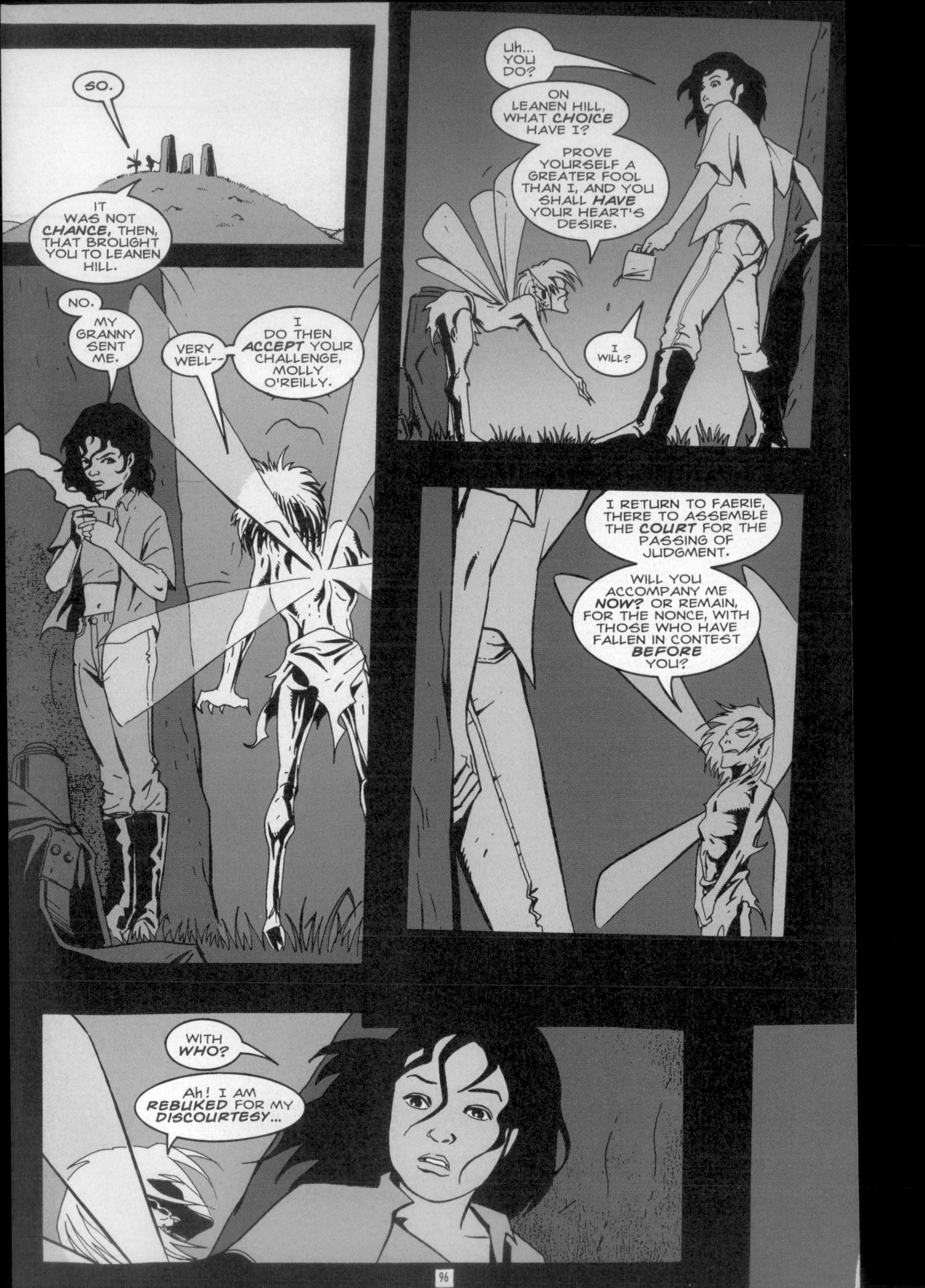
SO.
IT WAS NOT CHANCE, THEN, THAT BROUGHT YOU TO LEANEN HILL.
NO.
MY GRANNY SENT ME.
VERY WELL--
I DO THEN ACCEPT YOUR CHALLENGE, MOLLY O'REILLY.
Uh... YOU DO?
ON LEANEN HILL, WHAT CHOICE HAVE I?
PROVE YOURSELF A GREATER FOOL THAN I, AND YOU SHALL HAVE YOUR HEART'S DESIRE.
I WILL?
I RETURN TO FAERIE, THERE TO ASSEMBLE THE COURT FOR THE PASSING OF JUDGMENT.
WILL YOU ACCOMPANY ME NOW? OR REMAIN, FOR THE NONCE, WITH THOSE WHO HAVE FALLEN IN CONTEST BEFORE YOU?
WITH WHO?
Ah! I AM REBUKED FOR MY DISCOURTESY...

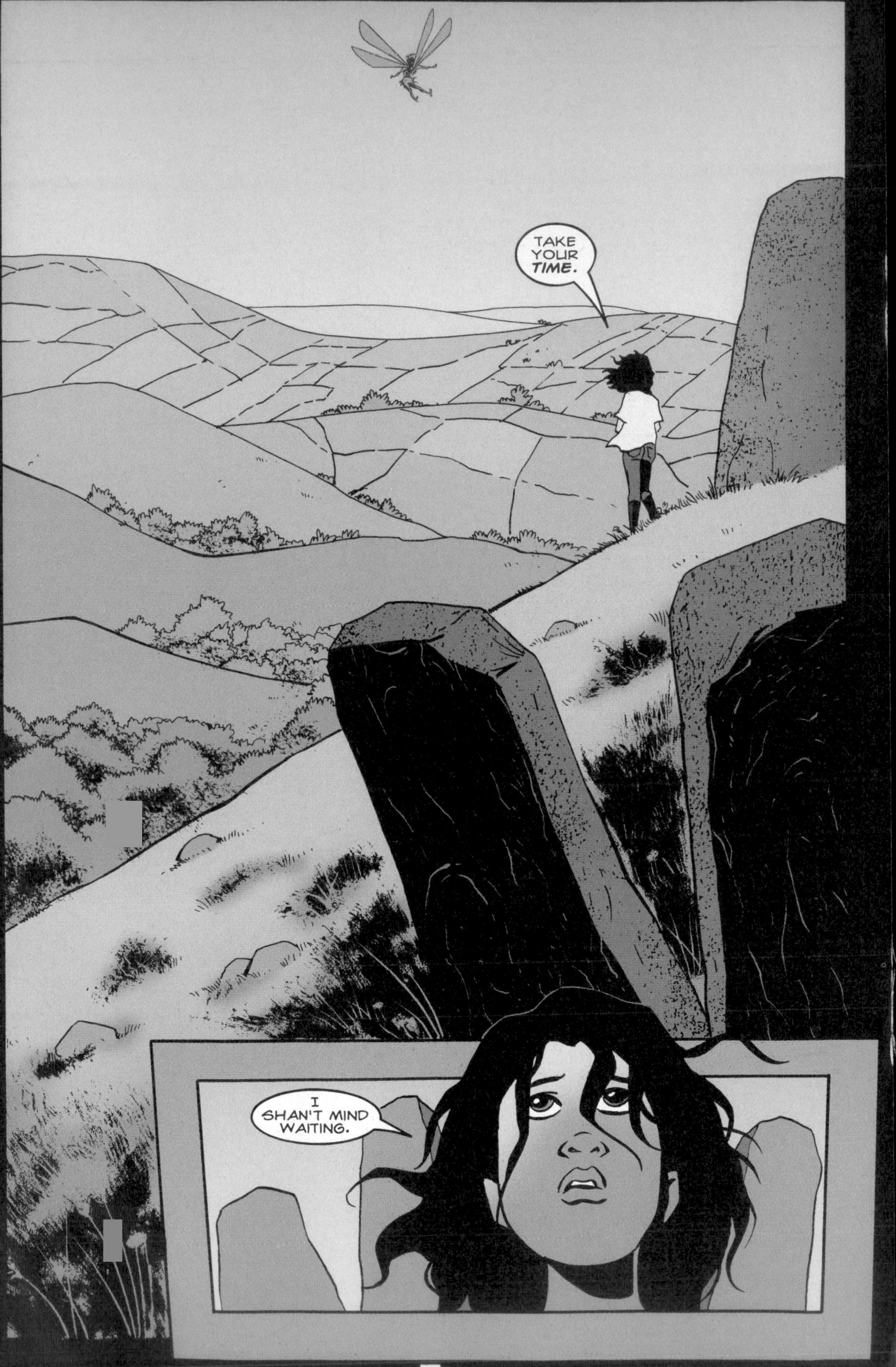
TAKE YOUR TIME.
I SHAN'T MIND WAITING.

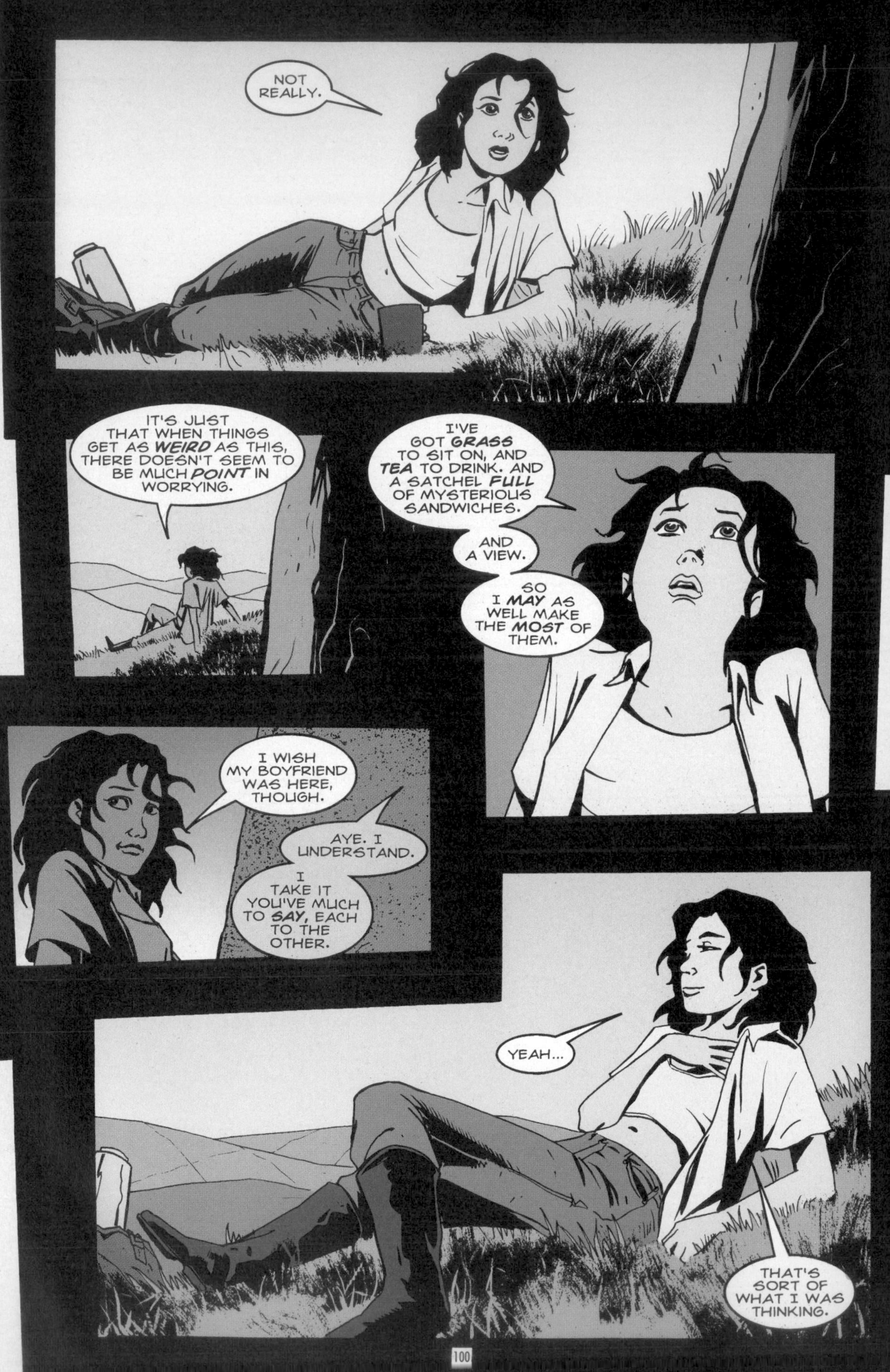
NOT REALLY.
IT'S JUST THAT WHEN THINGS GET AS WEIRD AS THIS, THERE DOESN'T SEEM TO BE MUCH POINT IN WORRYING.
I'VE GOT GRASS TO SIT ON, AND TEA TO DRINK. AND A SATCHEL FULL OF MYSTERIOUS SANDWICHES.
AND A VIEW.
SO I MAY AS WELL MAKE THE MOST OF THEM.
I WISH MY BOYFRIEND WAS HERE, THOUGH.
AYE. I UNDERSTAND.
I TAKE IT YOU'VE MUCH TO SAY, EACH TO THE OTHER.
YEAH...
THAT'S SORT OF WHAT I WAS THINKING.

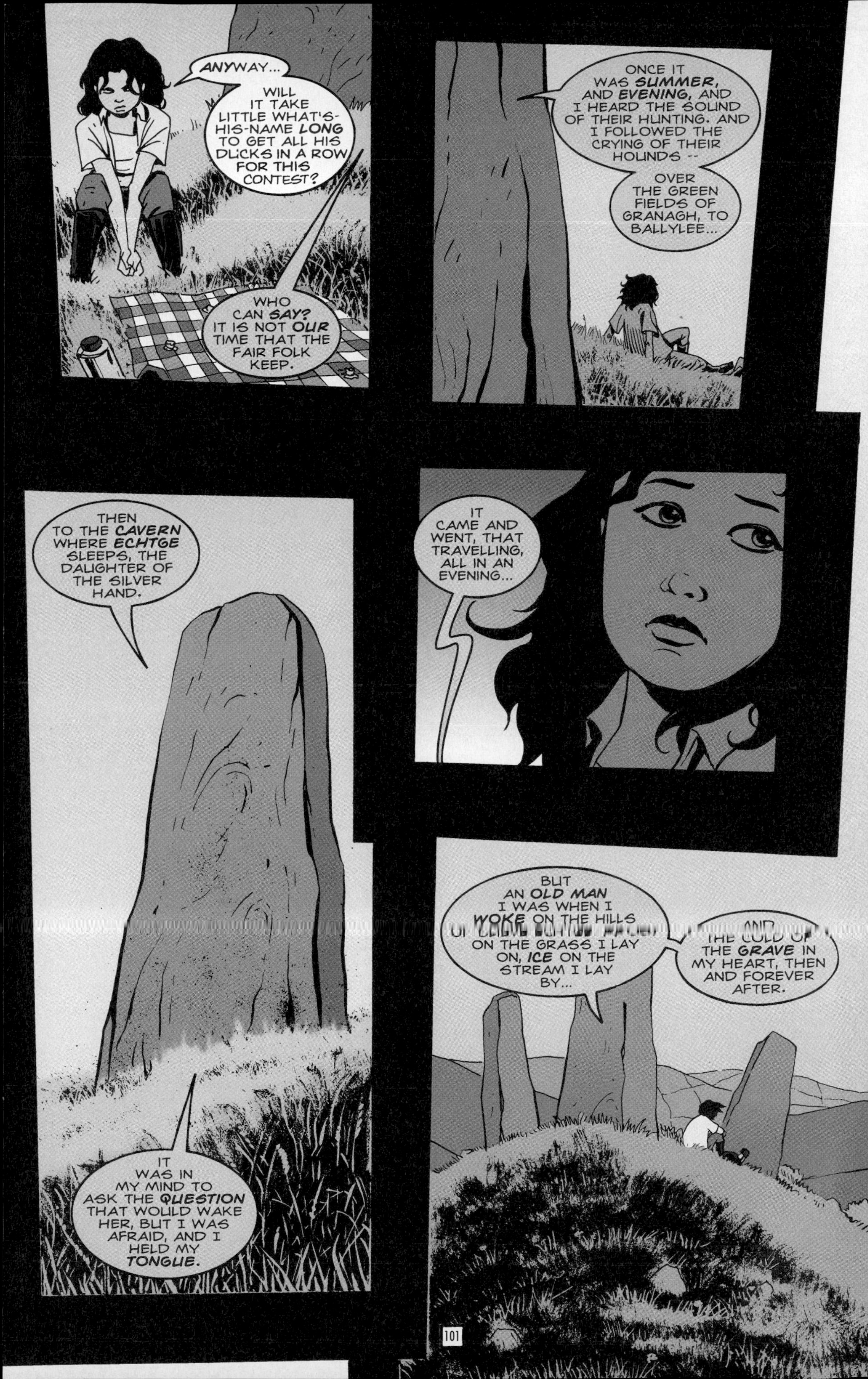
ANYWAY...
WILL IT TAKE LITTLE WHAT'S-HIS-NAME LONG TO GET ALL HIS DUCKS IN A ROW FOR THIS CONTEST?
WHO CAN SAY? IT IS NOT OUR TIME THAT THE FAIR FOLK KEEP.
ONCE IT WAS SUMMER, AND EVENING, AND I HEARD THE SOUND OF THEIR HUNTING. AND I FOLLOWED THE CRYING OF THEIR HOUNDS --
OVER THE GREEN FIELDS OF GRANAGH, TO BALLYLEE...
THEN TO THE CAVERN WHERE ECHTGE SLEEPS, THE DAUGHTER OF THE SILVER HAND.
IT WAS IN MY MIND TO ASK THE QUESTION THAT WOULD WAKE HER, BUT I WAS AFRAID, AND I HELD MY TONGUE.
IT CAME AND WENT, THAT TRAVELLING, ALL IN AN EVENING...
BUT AN OLD MAN I WAS WHEN I WOKE ON THE HILLS
ON THE GRASS I LAY ON, ICE ON THE STREAM I LAY BY...
AND THE COLD OF THE GRAVE IN MY HEART, THEN AND FOREVER AFTER.

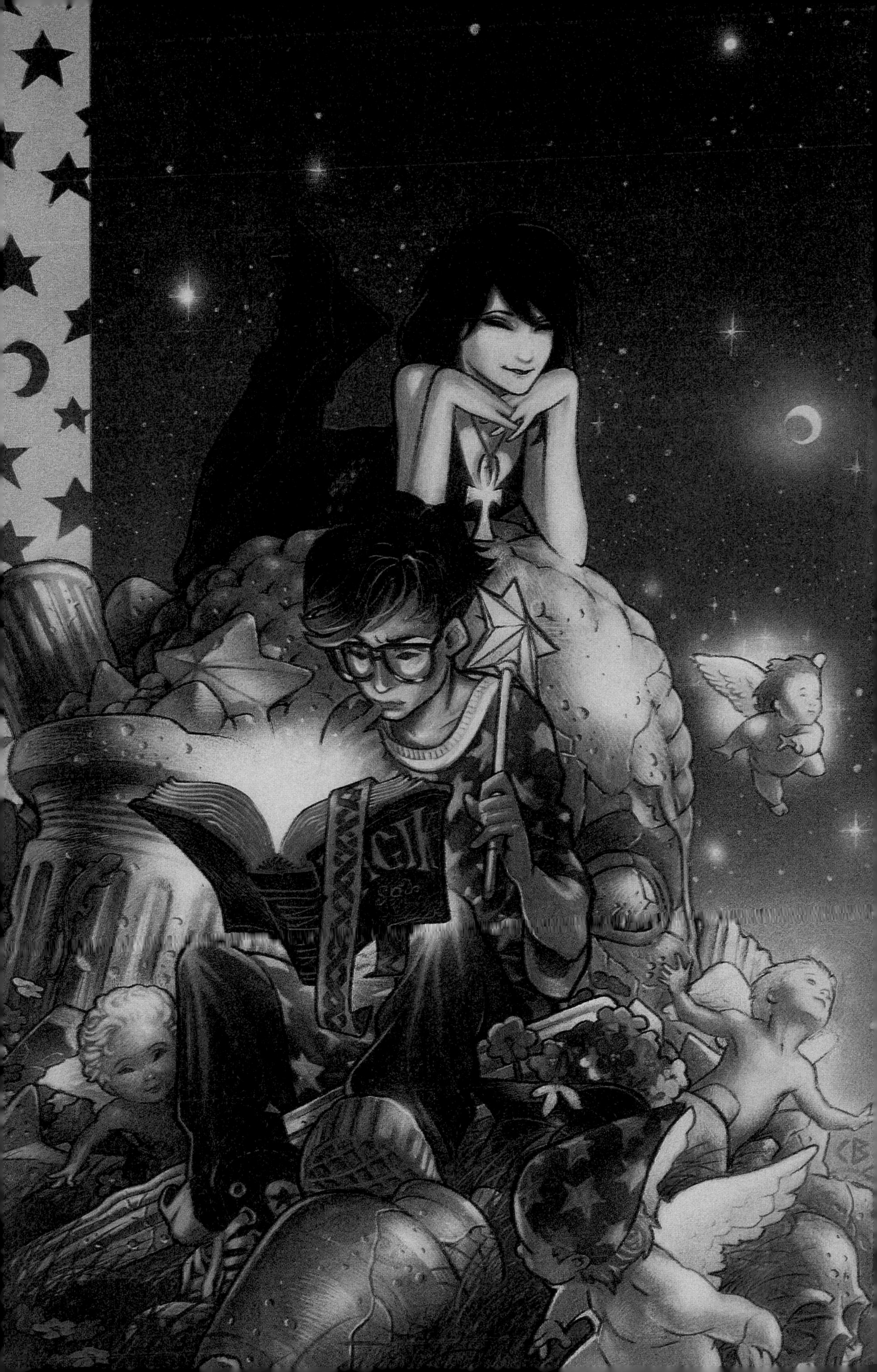

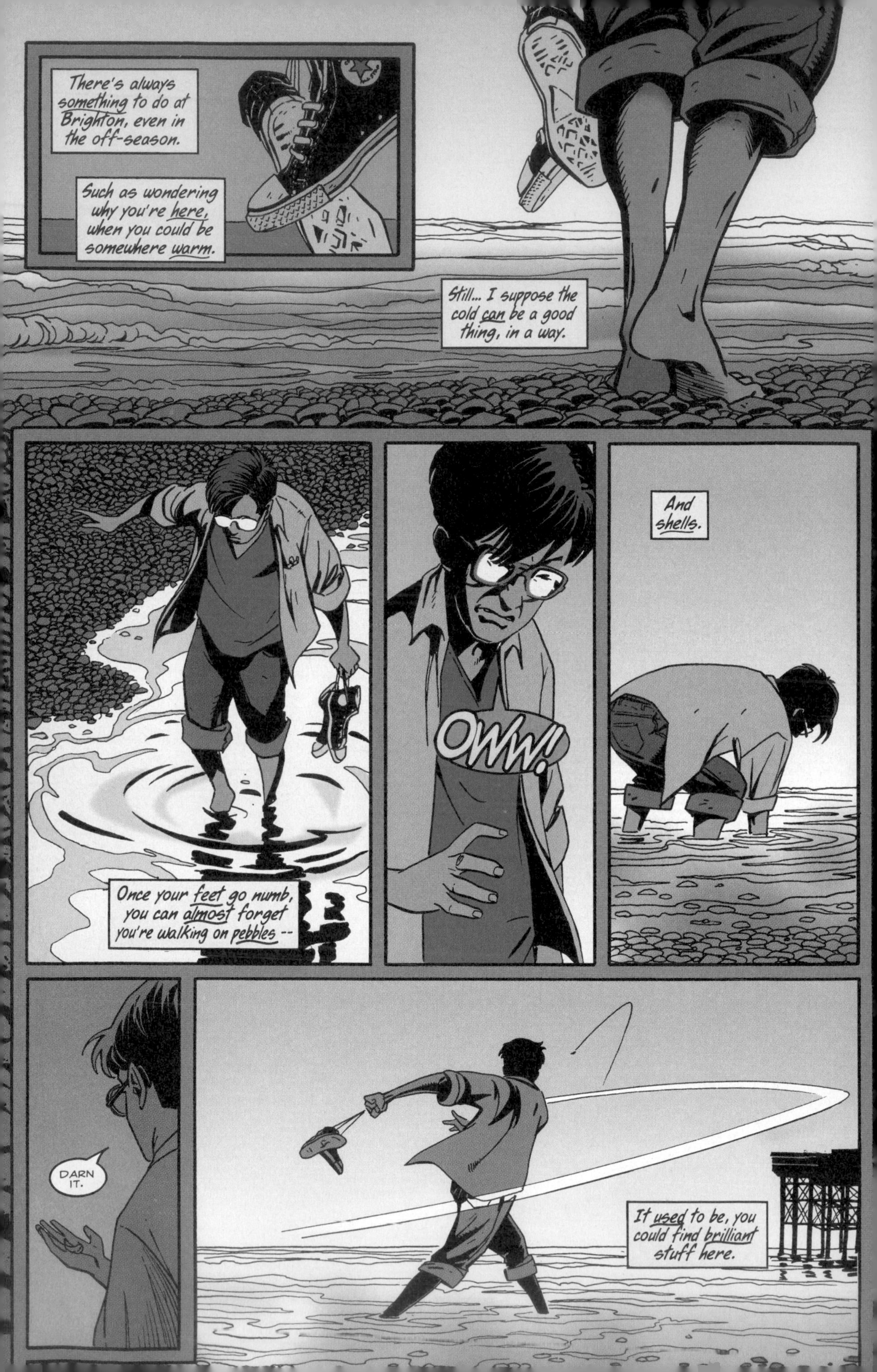

There's always something to do at Brighton, even in the off-season.
Such as wondering why you're here, when you could be somewhere warm.
Still... I suppose the cold can be a good thing, in a way.
Once your feet go numb, you can almost forget you're walking on pebbles --
OWW!
And shells.
DARN IT.
It used to be, you could find brilliant stuff here.

Now it's all just _bits_ of things.

Pieces --

Pieces and rain.

SO IS IT JUST _ME_, JIMMY -- OR WAS IT BETTER WHEN WE WERE KIDS?

WE DIDN'T CARE HOW COLD THE WATER WAS, BACK THEN.

NOT THAT IT WAS EVER THIS COLD.

DO YOU STILL GET COLD?

SINCE SLAGGINGHAM TURNED YOU INTO A _THING_?

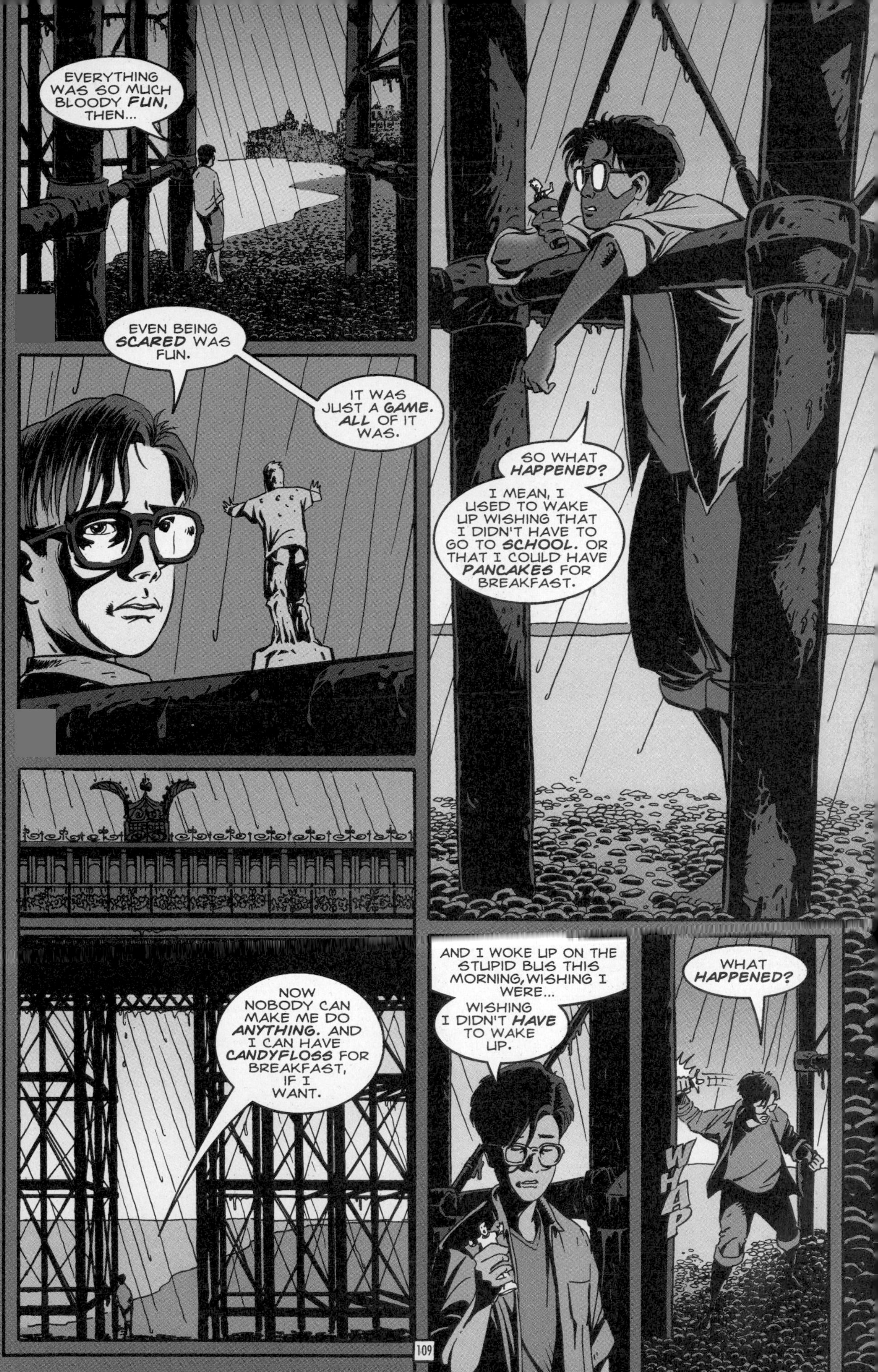
EVERYTHING WAS SO MUCH BLOODY FUN, THEN...
EVEN BEING SCARED WAS FUN.
IT WAS JUST A GAME. ALL OF IT WAS.
SO WHAT HAPPENED?
I MEAN, I USED TO WAKE UP WISHING THAT I DIDN'T HAVE TO GO TO SCHOOL. OR THAT I COULD HAVE PANCAKES FOR BREAKFAST.
NOW NOBODY CAN MAKE ME DO ANYTHING. AND I CAN HAVE CANDYFLOSS FOR BREAKFAST, IF I WANT.
AND I WOKE UP ON THE STUPID BUS THIS MORNING, WISHING I WERE...
WISHING I DIDN'T HAVE TO WAKE UP.
WHAT HAPPENED?
WHAP

SPIFF! IT'S A *CRUX* AN-SOMETHING -- LIKE THE *SPIDER MUMMY* USED TO ZAP *SCARAB-MAN* IN *PYRAMID OF EYES.*

CAN I *HAVE* IT?

I'LL *TRADE* YOU A *KNIGHT* IN *ARMOR* FOR IT.

REALLY?

I DON'T KNOW... WE HARDLY *EVER* PLAY KNIGHTS ANYMORE.

EXCUSE ME --

WELL... *YEAH.* ONLY NOT THE ONE WITH THE *MORNINGSTAR.*

COULDN'T HELP *OVERHEARING.* NO FAULT OF MY OWN. HEARING AID, YOU KNOW.

SKINNER'S THE NAME. J. ALFRED SKINNER.

SWAP YOU THE *FUNLAND* FOR THIS LITTLE BEAUTY.

RIDES, RIDES, *RIDES.* ALL DAY. FOR *FREE.*

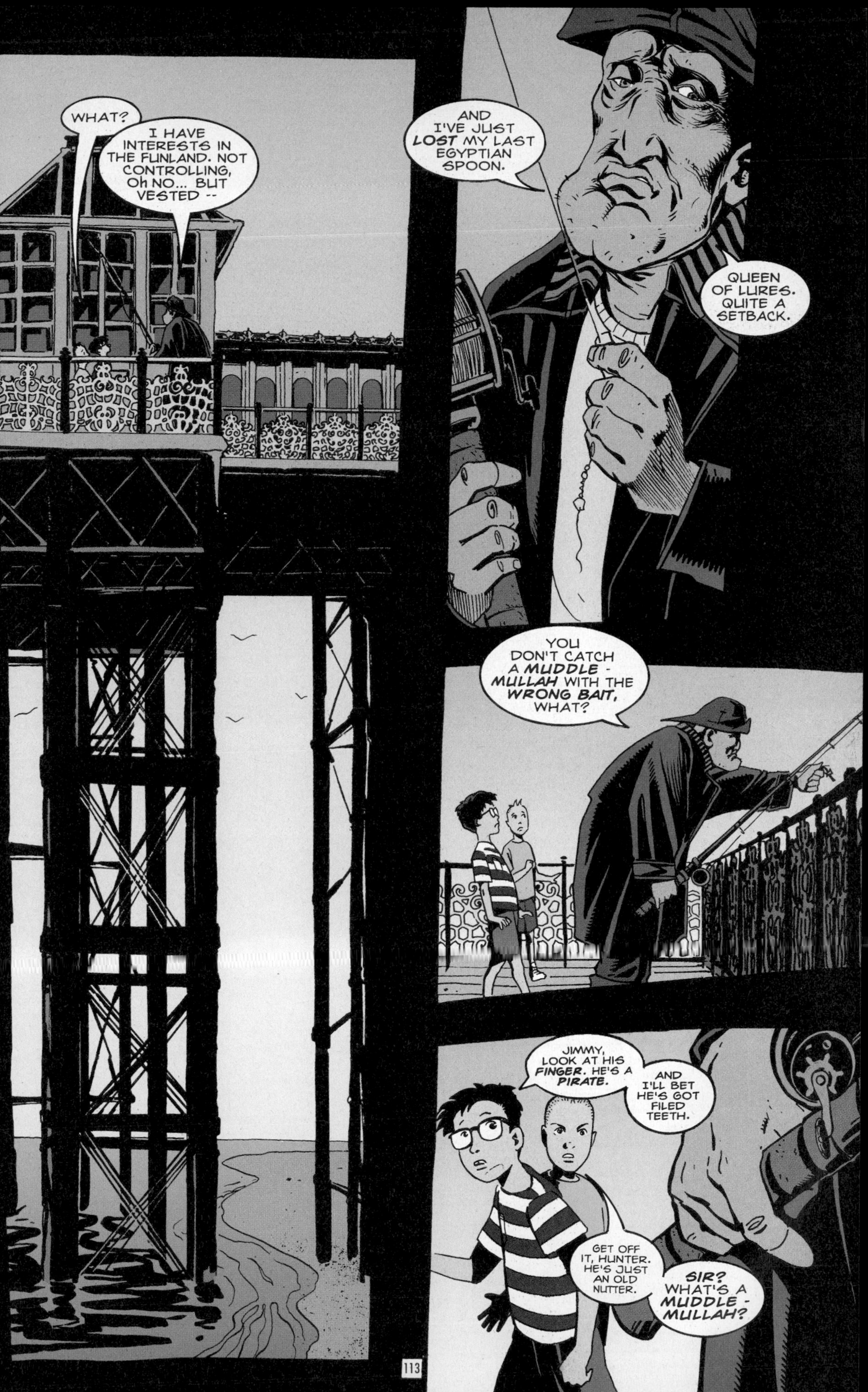
WHAT?
I HAVE INTERESTS IN THE FUNLAND. NOT CONTROLLING, Oh NO... BUT VESTED --
AND I'VE JUST LOST MY LAST EGYPTIAN SPOON.
QUEEN OF LURES. QUITE A SETBACK.
YOU DON'T CATCH A MUDDLE - MULLAH WITH THE WRONG BAIT, WHAT?
JIMMY, LOOK AT HIS FINGER. HE'S A PIRATE.
AND I'LL BET HE'S GOT FILED TEETH.
GET OFF IT, HUNTER. HE'S JUST AN OLD NUTTER.
SIR? WHAT'S A MUDDLE - MULLAH?

ARCHFIEND, OF THE WATERY ABYSS. TREPIDATION INCARNATE.

NASTY OLD THING.

SINKS HIS CLAWS INTO YOU *ONCE*, AND YOU'RE *HIS*. FOREVER.

UNLESS YOU CAN *RAISE HIM* FROM THE DEEPS AGAIN. AND *SPIT* IN HIS BLOODY *EYE*.

YOU CAN *HAVE* THE CRUX THINGIE, MISTER SKINNER. BUT JIMMY AND I HAVE TO GO NOW.

HAR. THINK I'M *MAD*, EH? *POTTY.* "AN OLD NUTTER." "WITH FILED TEETH."

COME ON, HUNTER. WE'RE NOT SUPPOSED TO TALK TO STRANGERS --

ARE YOU A PIRATE?

I'M *AFRAID* OF THE SEA, BOY. AND EVERYTHING ELSE.

HERE. YOUR TICKETS. *RIDE.*

HAR. *GOT IT*, DON'T YOU? THE *LUCK*. I FEEL IT --

YOLI, *YOU'LL* BE THE ONE...

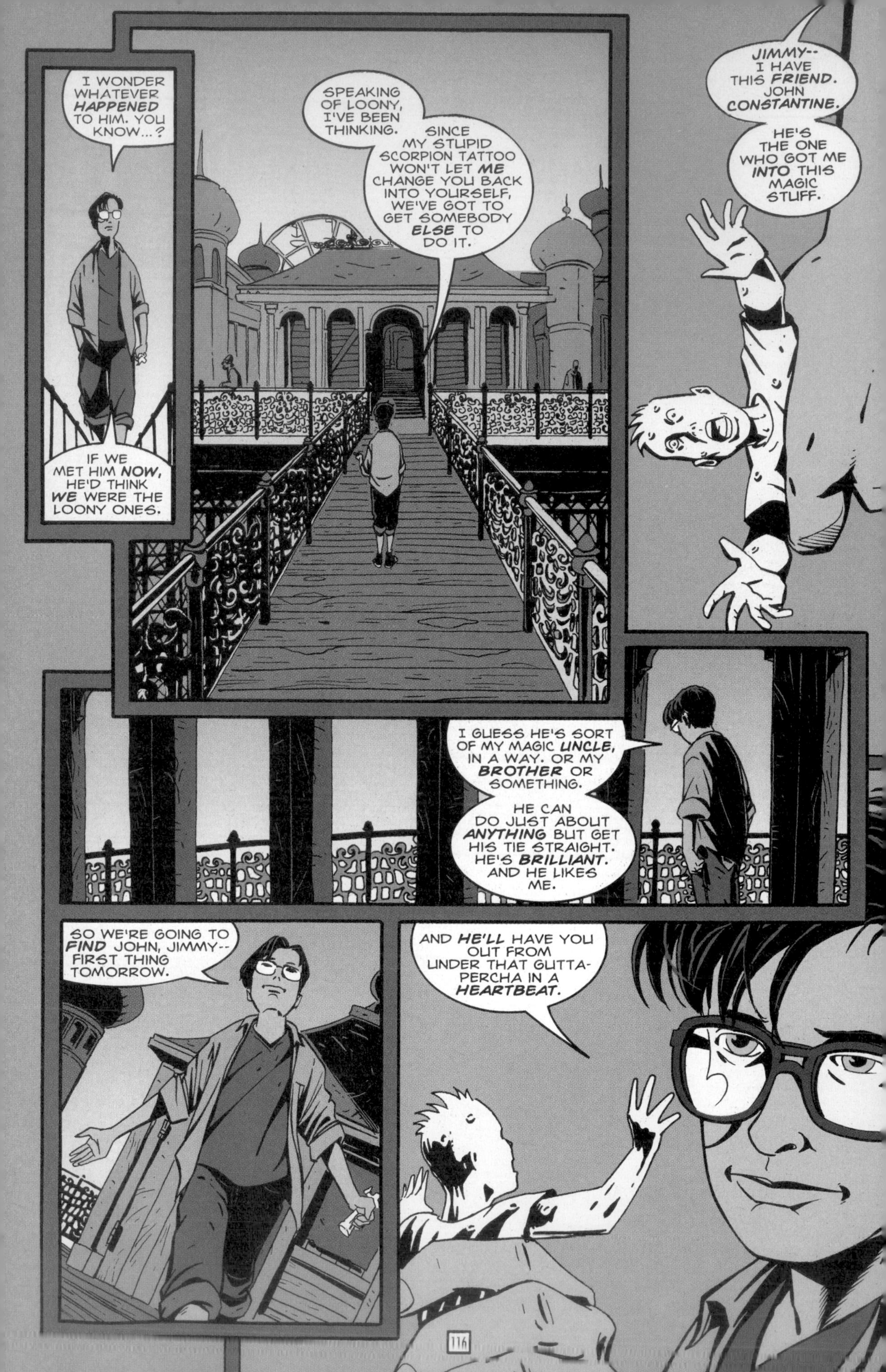
I WONDER WHATEVER HAPPENED TO HIM. YOU KNOW...?
IF WE MET HIM NOW, HE'D THINK WE WERE THE LOONY ONES.
SPEAKING OF LOONY, I'VE BEEN THINKING.
SINCE MY STUPID SCORPION TATTOO WON'T LET ME CHANGE YOU BACK INTO YOURSELF, WE'VE GOT TO GET SOMEBODY ELSE TO DO IT.
JIMMY-- I HAVE THIS FRIEND. JOHN CONSTANTINE.
HE'S THE ONE WHO GOT ME INTO THIS MAGIC STUFF.
I GUESS HE'S SORT OF MY MAGIC UNCLE, IN A WAY. OR MY BROTHER OR SOMETHING.
HE CAN DO JUST ABOUT ANYTHING BUT GET HIS TIE STRAIGHT. HE'S BRILLIANT. AND HE LIKES ME.
SO WE'RE GOING TO FIND JOHN, JIMMY-- FIRST THING TOMORROW.
AND HE'LL HAVE YOU OUT FROM UNDER THAT GUTTA-PERCHA IN A HEARTBEAT.

AND MAYBE I CAN *STAY* WITH HIM, AFTER THAT --

AND I CAN *HELP HIM* WITH THINGS --

AND HE CAN *TEACH* ME THINGS.

IT'S ABOUT *TIME* SOMEONE TAUGHT ME *SOMETHING.*

DAD. WORRYING ABOUT *ME.* HAH.

AND...

I DON'T THINK DAD AND GWEN WOULD... *WORRY,* IF THEY KNEW THAT JOHN WAS... TAKING *CARE* OF ME.

COME ON, JIMMY --

LET'S GO UP ON THE FERRIS WHEEL AGAIN --

LAST ONE *THERE* IS A ROTTEN EGG.

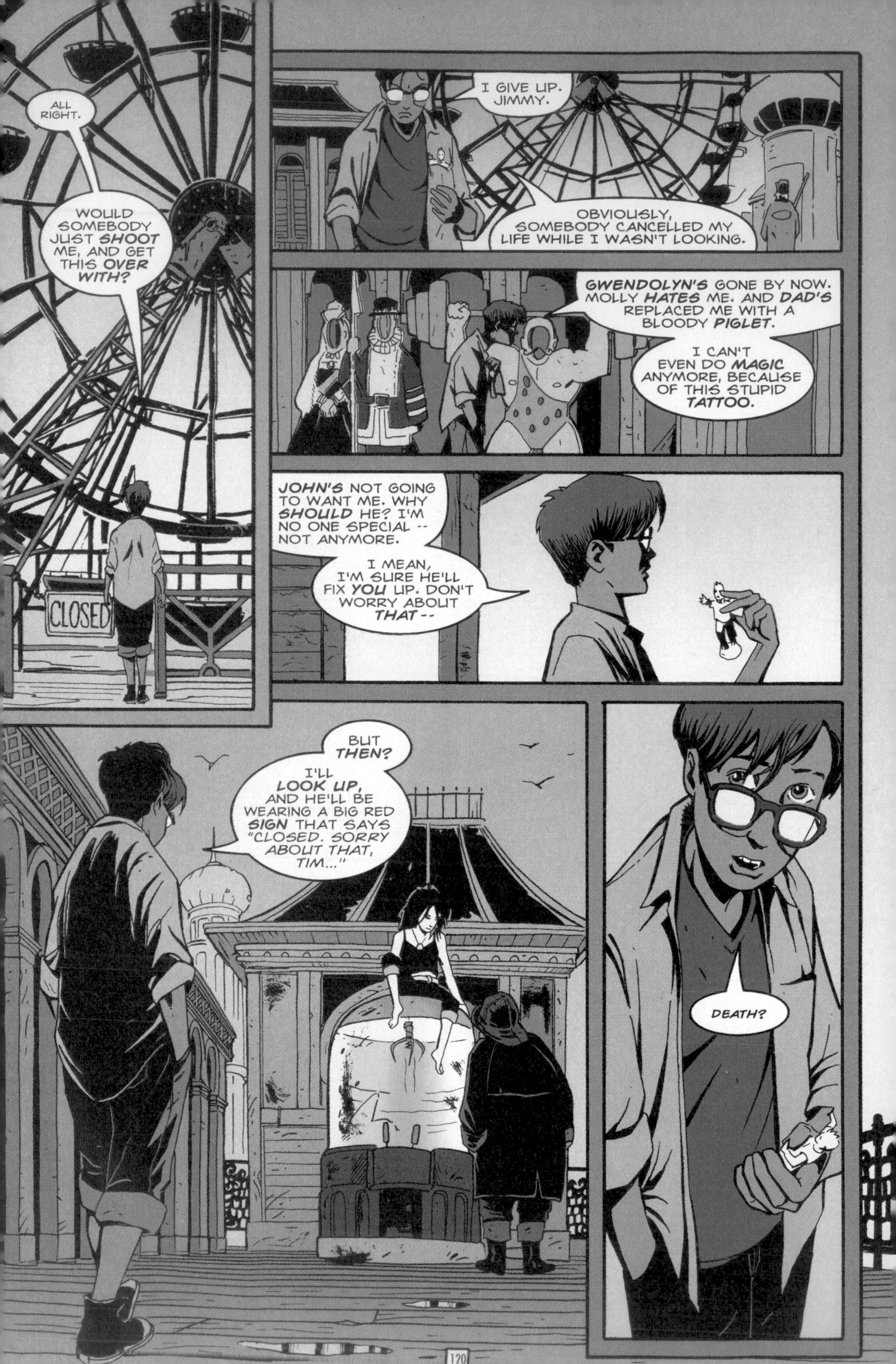
ALL RIGHT.
WOULD SOMEBODY JUST SHOOT ME, AND GET THIS OVER WITH?
CLOSED
I GIVE UP. JIMMY.
OBVIOUSLY, SOMEBODY CANCELLED MY LIFE WHILE I WASN'T LOOKING.
GWENDOLYN'S GONE BY NOW. MOLLY HATES ME. AND DAD'S REPLACED ME WITH A BLOODY PIGLET.
I CAN'T EVEN DO MAGIC ANYMORE, BECAUSE OF THIS STUPID TATTOO.
JOHN'S NOT GOING TO WANT ME. WHY SHOULD HE? I'M NO ONE SPECIAL -- NOT ANYMORE.
I MEAN, I'M SURE HE'LL FIX YOU UP. DON'T WORRY ABOUT THAT --
BUT THEN?
I'LL LOOK UP, AND HE'LL BE WEARING A BIG RED SIGN THAT SAYS "CLOSED. SORRY ABOUT THAT, TIM..."
DEATH?

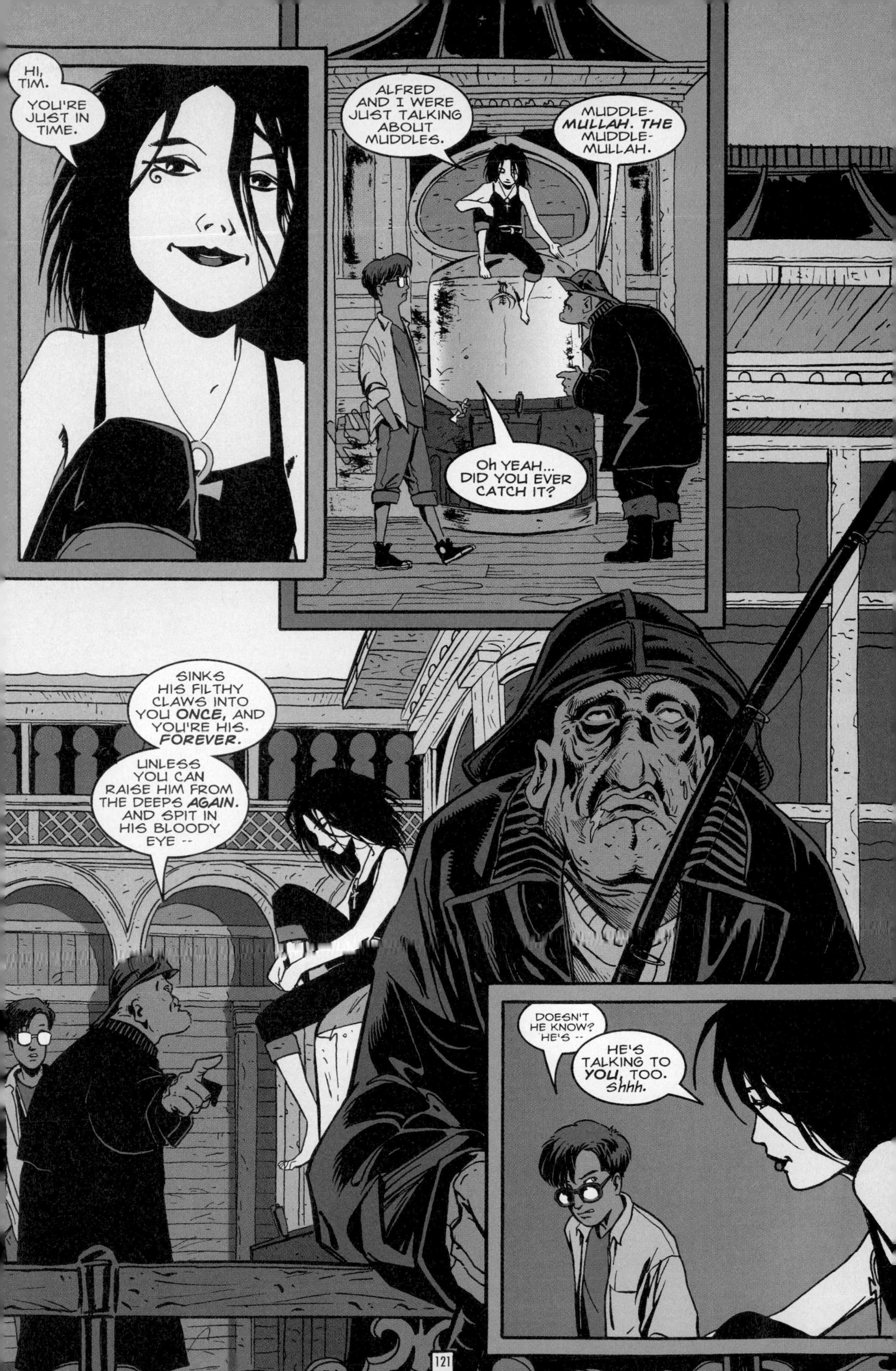
HI, TIM.
YOU'RE JUST IN TIME.
ALFRED AND I WERE JUST TALKING ABOUT MUDDLES.
MUDDLE-MULLAH. THE MUDDLE-MULLAH.
Oh YEAH... DID YOU EVER CATCH IT?
SINKS HIS FILTHY CLAWS INTO YOU ONCE, AND YOU'RE HIS. FOREVER.
UNLESS YOU CAN RAISE HIM FROM THE DEEPS AGAIN. AND SPIT IN HIS BLOODY EYE --
DOESN'T HE KNOW? HE'S --
HE'S TALKING TO YOU, TOO. Shhh.

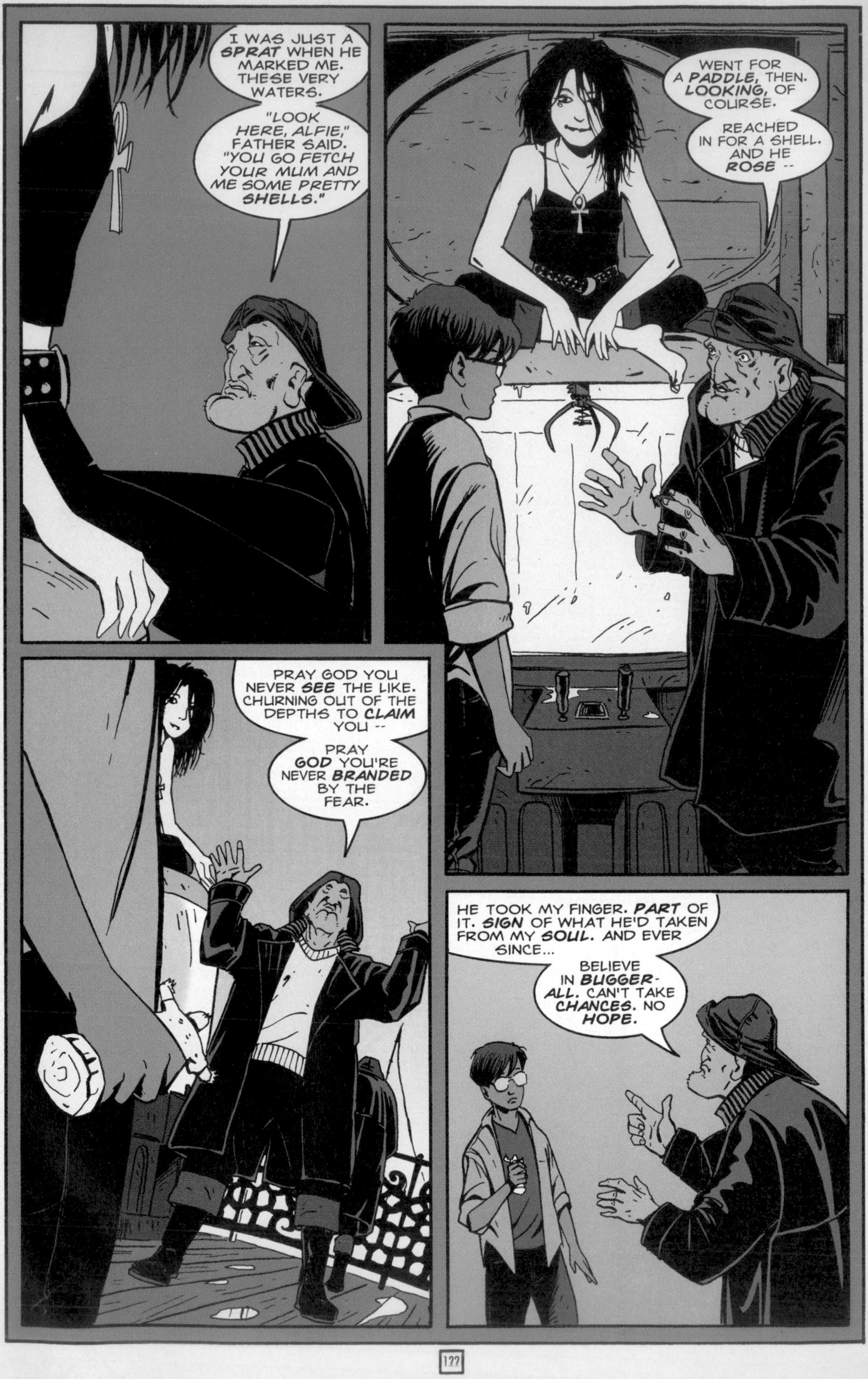
I WAS JUST A SPRAT WHEN HE MARKED ME. THESE VERY WATERS.
"LOOK HERE, ALFIE," FATHER SAID. "YOU GO FETCH YOUR MUM AND ME SOME PRETTY SHELLS."
WENT FOR A PADDLE, THEN. LOOKING, OF COURSE.
REACHED IN FOR A SHELL. AND HE ROSE --
PRAY GOD YOU NEVER SEE THE LIKE. CHURNING OUT OF THE DEPTHS TO CLAIM YOU --
PRAY GOD YOU'RE NEVER BRANDED BY THE FEAR.
HE TOOK MY FINGER. PART OF IT. SIGN OF WHAT HE'D TAKEN FROM MY SOUL. AND EVER SINCE...
BELIEVE IN BUGGER-ALL. CAN'T TAKE CHANCES. NO HOPE.

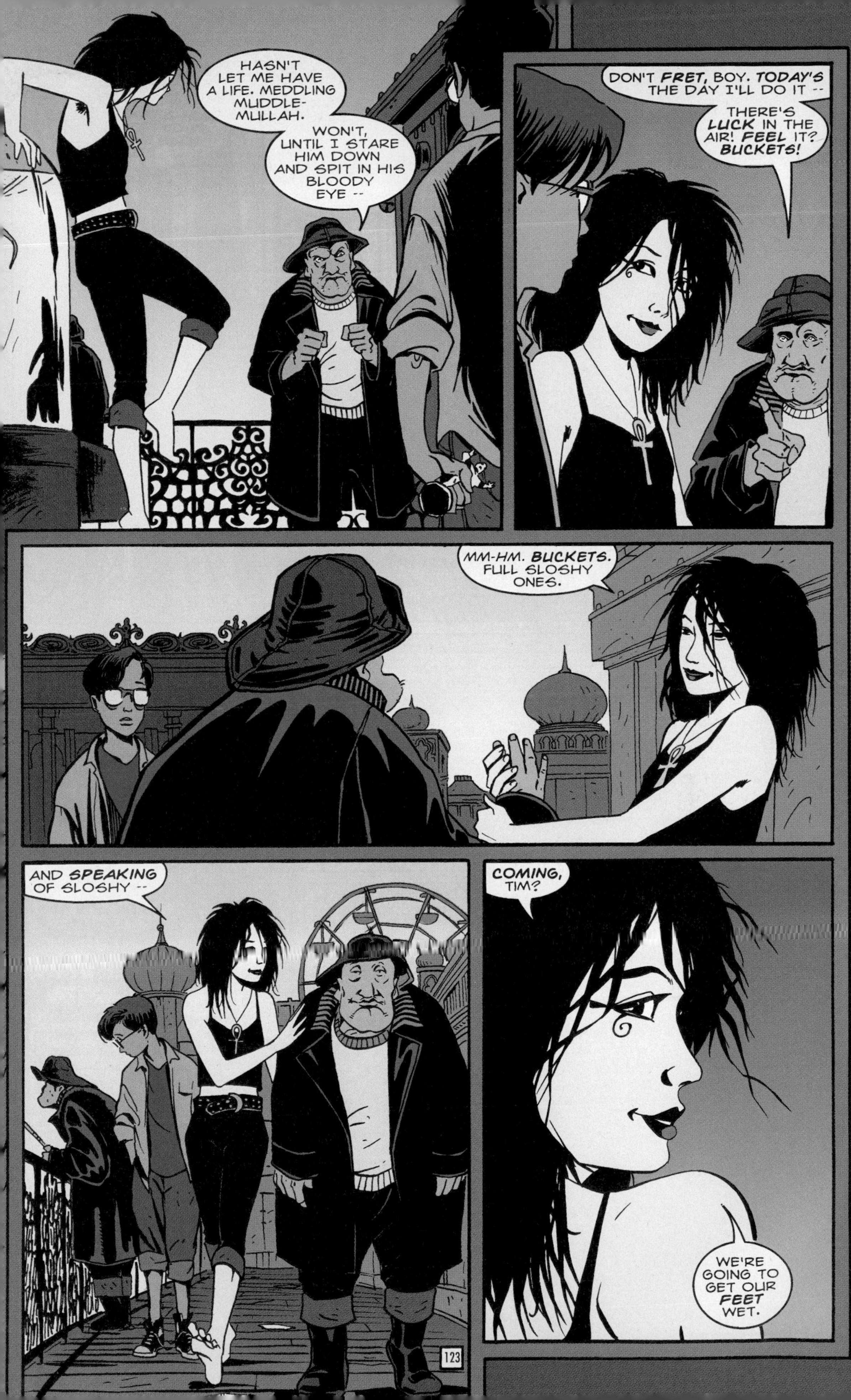
HASN'T LET ME HAVE A LIFE. MEDDLING MUDDLE-MULLAH.
WON'T, UNTIL I STARE HIM DOWN AND SPIT IN HIS BLOODY EYE --
DON'T FRET, BOY. TODAY'S THE DAY I'LL DO IT --
THERE'S LUCK IN THE AIR! FEEL IT? BUCKETS!
MM-HM. BUCKETS. FULL SLOSHY ONES.
AND SPEAKING OF SLOSHY --
COMING, TIM?
WE'RE GOING TO GET OUR FEET WET.

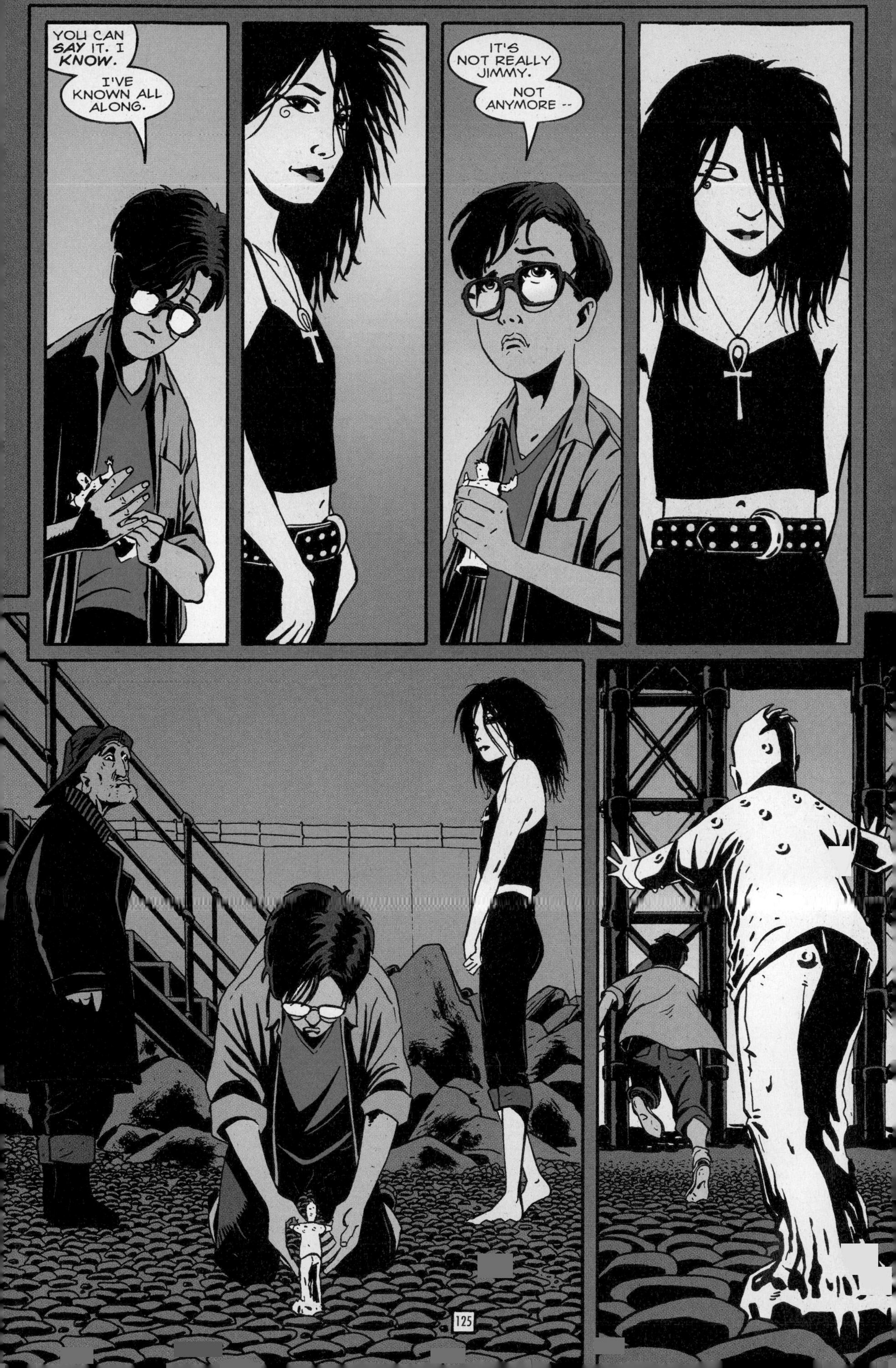
YOU CAN SAY IT. I KNOW.
I'VE KNOWN ALL ALONG.
IT'S NOT REALLY JIMMY.
NOT ANYMORE --

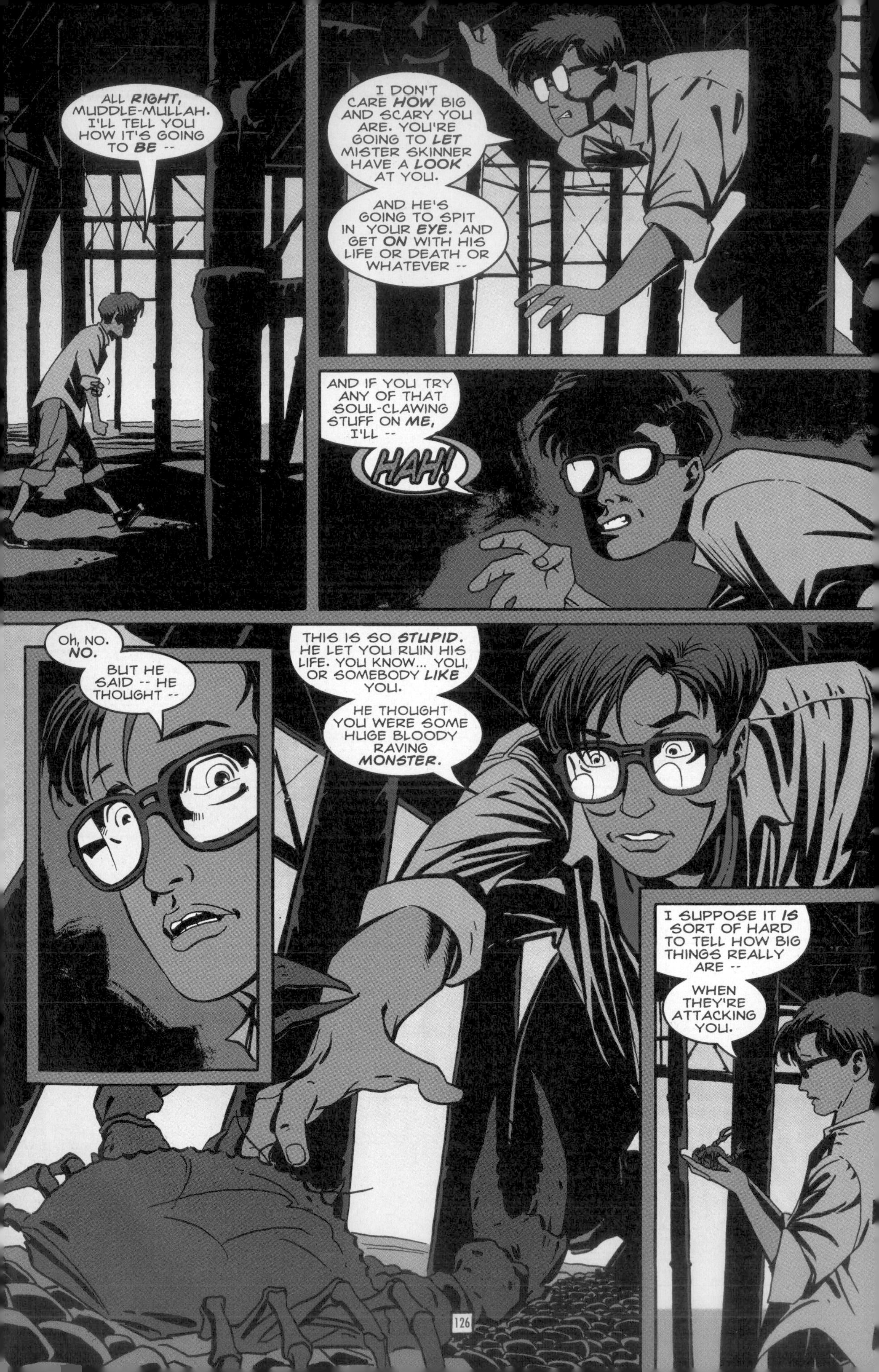
ALL RIGHT, MUDDLE-MULLAH. I'LL TELL YOU HOW IT'S GOING TO BE --
I DON'T CARE HOW BIG AND SCARY YOU ARE. YOU'RE GOING TO LET MISTER SKINNER HAVE A LOOK AT YOU.
AND HE'S GOING TO SPIT IN YOUR EYE. AND GET ON WITH HIS LIFE OR DEATH OR WHATEVER --
AND IF YOU TRY ANY OF THAT SOUL-CLAWING STUFF ON ME, I'LL --
HAH!
Oh, NO. NO.
BUT HE SAID -- HE THOUGHT --
THIS IS SO STUPID. HE LET YOU RUIN HIS LIFE. YOU KNOW... YOU, OR SOMEBODY LIKE YOU.
HE THOUGHT YOU WERE SOME HUGE BLOODY RAVING MONSTER.
I SUPPOSE IT IS SORT OF HARD TO TELL HOW BIG THINGS REALLY ARE --
WHEN THEY'RE ATTACKING YOU.

Darkness and Dreams!

Contemporary Graphic Novels From TITAN BOOKS!